I'm Not
ANYONE

To Sulla

your the Friend!

I'm Not
ANYONE

A Story of Reinvention and Acceptance

ROGER P. GIMBEL, EDP

First Edition

ISBN: 978-0-578-32595-8 (print)
ISBN: 978-0-578-32596-5 (ebook)

Book and cover design by *www.wordzworth.com*

Dedicated to my parents, may their memory be for a blessing and their legacy live on for generations.

Herman L. (Hy) Gimbel & Audrey M. Gimbel

Their unwavering encouragement and guidance,
love and support are evident in all my endeavors.

The proceeds of this volume will be donated to a scholarship fund in their name which will award higher education grants to deserving students committed to a career in the document management and graphic communications marketplace.

CONTENTS

INTRODUCTION

My name is Roger Gimbel. I'm well known in the printing industry; that's no surprise, since I've been in the printing business in one way or another for about sixty years. My father was a printer, and I still consider myself a printer. Even though the days of getting ink under my fingernails are long past, I still spend my days working with printers and advising companies with in-house print centers. I'm always talking about print, and consulting with vendors in the printing industry.

People see me as a successful businessman who has clients and connections across the globe. They think I've got things totally under control. Business deals are constantly brewing. My phone is always ringing, I'm in demand as a speaker and presenter, and I'm constantly on the go. I own a beautiful boat that takes me on long ocean voyages when I find time to get away for a while.

I guess that describes my life pretty well today, but it wasn't always that way. Oh no — I spent a good deal of my youth trying NOT to be a traditional businessman. I came of age in the sixties, and it wasn't cool to be an obvious participant in the establishment, man!

I had long hair, rode motorcycles, and concentrated on having the time of my life — a typical teenager, I guess. The world was changing dramatically when I graduated from high school, and I made sure I included myself in the exciting events that were happening all around me.

With my father running a print business and as a high school kid who needed some walking around money, I naturally worked part time in the print shop. I was learning the business from the ground up — literally. I swept the floors!

In one of my first jobs, I was a stripper. Wait, that doesn't sound right. I wasn't *that* wild as a young man! In printing, a stripper works with the film negatives, getting them ready to make printing plates. That's what I did. With my clothes on.

We were a full-service shop that served customers from concept to completion. Our services included typesetting, layout, design, binding, and shipping.

As I worked in the shop, I grew to love the printing business. I admired my father, who was an innovator and grew his business from practically nothing to a thriving enterprise. He was a visionary and frequently had prototype machines in his shop, providing equipment manufacturers with valuable pre-release information about their products.

I knew I wanted to do something with the printing business, but I always had the idea that I could come up with my own innovations. I didn't know what they were at the time, but I was confident that I would someday make a name for myself on my own.

Perhaps the time period had something to do with it. I can remember feeling like a revolutionary. Society was evolving and the young people were driving the changes. Anything seemed possible because so many things that were previously thought impossible were already occurring.

Think about all the things that happened just in 1969, the year I graduated from high school. We landed on the moon and the Concord supersonic airliner took to the sky. Huge outdoor rock music festivals were attracting hundreds of thousands of people (I was there – more on that later). Large protests of the Vietnam war were happening. Young men like me worried about the draft, and women were burning their bras. The viciousness of the Charles Manson murders in California shocked the nation and the Chicago Seven trial about the riots at the Democratic National Convention the previous summer had begun

(I knew some of those guys). Bell-bottom jeans and tie-dyed t-shirts were the uniform of youth. Drug use, the birth control pill, and rock music contributed to a culture of freedom never experienced by so many at once.

Growing up in this time in history influenced how I conducted myself for many years as a young man, trying to make my mark on the world and decide what I wanted to do with my life. Some things I did and some people I met may surprise you.

As I grew older, my focus changed dramatically and not always by choice. Over the last many decades, this more mature persona is probably what people imagine when they think of Roger Gimbel. But that's not the way things started for me, and I firmly believe my life today would be much different had I not explored all the options available to me in my younger days.

I'm thankful I had those experiences. I wouldn't change anything if given the opportunity to do it all again. Without the crazy business ventures and hustle and drive it took to move from one adventure to the next, my life would have been less fulfilling.

Some things that happened to me weren't very nice. I eventually had to sell the family business to a group of people who were not the upstanding businesspeople I thought they were. That's the takeover part of this book and we'll get to that.

The takeover could have destroyed me professionally. It nearly did for a while, leaving me for the first time in my life with a sense of being adrift — an ironic feeling for someone for whom boating was an important part of my life!

All my experiences leading up to the takeover influenced how I reacted and what I decided to do about it. Looking back on the choices I made as a young person and a budding businessman, I now realize how valuable all those experiences were when I was suddenly without a job or a real plan.

This book is a story of my life's journey. I took some purposeful steps along the way and some things I left to chance, with mixed results. Other times, events were forced upon me. At points in my life, I felt I wasn't anyone. I had doubts about my worth, and where I was headed. All these things have combined to influence the kind of businessman and human being I have become.

What inspired me to write this chronicle? In one sense, it's an autobiography — a description of notable events in my life. Some of which are outrageous and have been amusing fodder for many dinner conversations. In another way, this book is a history of my career, including an assortment of colorful characters that encouraged and supported me. It's also about where I started and how I developed expertise in the print industry.

What I did not realize until I finished is that this story is about how great successes, as well as many adversities, meld together in just the way they were meant to be. They don't exist without each other. I was fortunate to spot and seize upon some amazing opportunities. I also failed to recognize some pitfalls. This is a record of how I arrived at where I am and what drives me to continue moving forward. Perhaps you will see in here something that helps you to avoid a pothole or inspires you to reach for a great brass ring along your way.

It's a remarkable story and one that few people have ever heard. I hope you find it interesting.

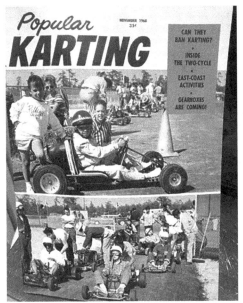

Sister *Gail*, me in the go cart, and our cousin *Stuart*

Me and my dad on a party boat

the *Lady Audrey Three*

1

. . .

1965 — 1978

College, Discos, and Toys

My father, Hy Gimbel, started his printing company, Madison Square Offset, in 1942. His brother, my uncle Harry, was his partner and they ran the business from a tiny office on Broadway in New York City. The space contained one small printing press, a phone, and little else. As the business grew, it was very much a family affair. Besides Harry, my uncle Phil, cousin Harriet, cousin Janis, Janis' husband George, and other family members all worked in the company at one time or another.

Before the print company, my immigrant father was a street vendor. He started from humble beginnings, but Hy Gimbel worked tirelessly to grow his printing business. He met people, made connections, and always kept an eye on what was happening in the marketplace.

As the company grew, the name changed to Electronic Reproduction Service, or ERS, as we always called it, and moved to the fourth floor of a building on West 25th Street. This is where I worked part time during my high school years.

When I wasn't working or going to school in the '60s, I spent time with my father at the Deep Sea Club, which later became the Montauk Yacht Club. Dad helped set up fishing tournaments for the club. It was my first introduction to the Montauk facility, a place that would be my boating home for decades.

Montauk was also where I met Frank Mundus, the shark guy. He later became the model for Robert Shaw's character, Quint in the movie "Jaws".

Mr. Mundus was known as Monster Man. He had a diamond and gold earring and a dagger with a shark-tooth blade. I was impressed.

Mundus later took Peter Benchley, the author of the best-seller "Jaws" out to sea several times. Mundus showed Benchley how he harpooned big sharks and attached barrels to tire them out. This became a major point of emphasis in Benchley's book and the movie that followed.

In the mid to late '60s my father wanted me to learn the printing trade, so that's what I did. I earned a few dollars from doing the work, which funded my other interests at the time — motorcycles and girlfriends.

In August 1969, right after graduating from high school, my girlfriend and I drove up to a place called White Lake, New York and camped out. We had tickets to a concert. After a while, it started getting really crowded. Top musical acts attracted nearly 400,000 people to The Woodstock Music and Art Fair. We stayed all three days at the event that most people recognize as the best example of America's youth counterculture of the 1960s.

I didn't know it at the time, but my sister Gail told me that when my father learned I was camped out at Woodstock among the hippies and drugs he threatened to drive to White Lake, rent a horse, and get me out of there. I guess the horse was for transportation since the roads were blocked with abandoned vehicles for miles around the event.

I met a lot of really interesting people at Woodstock. I became acquainted with Abbie Hoffman, who was involved with the Student Nonviolent Coordinating Committee (SNCC). Among other publicity stunts he pulled off in the late '60s, Hoffman famously interrupted a performance by rock band The Who at Woodstock to plead the case of an arrested White Panther leader.

I was, for a time, a member of the Students for a Democratic Society (SDS). The organization had a presence at Cornell University, where my girlfriend was going to college. Having met Bobby Seale of the Black Panthers, I eventually severed my SDS ties after they began associating with his group, who I believed had a much more violent agenda.

The government charged Hoffman, Jerry Rubin, and five others with conspiracy and crossing state lines to incite a riot as part of the famous Chicago Seven trial.

Black Panther Bobby Seale was the eighth defendant who disrupted the trial. He was eventually gagged and bound to a chair in the courtroom.

My college career began at Robert Morris University, one of a handful of "off the cuff" schools that accepted me. I was sort of a character — a "B" to "C" student at best. Somehow, I squeaked my way out of high school, but I graduated and got accepted to college. Though my family was in the printing business, my collegiate field of study had nothing to do with the industry.

The whole Woodstock experience, the cultural revolution, and the continuing Vietnam war were affecting my view of business and my vision of who I should be. Even though my dad was a self-made businessman and a successful entrepreneur, I wasn't too keen on following a traditional path through college and into business.

Unfortunately, along with agreeing with the "destroy the establishment" movement in principle, I also had a fondness for nice things. I liked cars, motorcycles, and nice clothes. The prevalent attitude among the youth of the time didn't really match up with having money. Today, I guess you'd say I was conflicted. Back then, I just knew that I had no idea about what I wanted to do or how I should shape my world.

I wasn't against bending the rules. While at college, I owned a nice motorcycle that I kept inside my apartment — with a full gas tank. If anyone found out, I would have certainly been asked to find somewhere else to live, but I wasn't really worried about it. I'd worked out a deal with the housekeeper to keep my motorcycle a secret.

During my first year at Robert Morris, my male friends and I all kept an eye on the military draft lottery. My number was 126. The word was the draft would not take anyone past 110, so it looked like I may not be chosen, but it was too close for comfort to me.

I remember sitting in a place called Gallatin Hall on campus with my long-haired friends, debating whether we wanted to stay in school. The college had made what seemed to be an attack on our freedom of expression. If we wanted to stay in school, we'd have to cut our hair! This just made everything worse. None of us was willing to get a haircut.

Nobody knew what to do. Should we stay and cut our hair? Get ourselves kicked out of school? Move to Canada to dodge the draft? Maybe it sounds silly to younger people who never lived through the overwhelming sense of unrest and dissatisfaction that was in the air. But for us eighteen- or nineteen-year-old kids, this was a huge deal. Nearly 12,000 soldiers died in Vietnam in 1969. Casualty numbers were reported on the news every night. None of us wanted to risk being one of them.

My dad shared my concern. He made arrangements with a printing company in Canada. Dad said I could work there if I decided to leave the country.

On top of all that stress about the war and haircuts, Robert Morris University had a relationship with several Arab countries. The student body included transfer students from United Arab Emirates and Kuwait. We had Kuwaiti students in the dorm where I lived. That was fine until my roommate and I walked into one of the Kuwaiti student rooms one night and saw the big flags that said "Kill the Jewish People". Considering we were both long-haired Jewish people, the decision about staying in school or leaving got a lot easier. I don't know if the Kuwaitis knew we were Jewish, but we sure did. We took to barricading our doors at night, just in case.

I called my parents and told them this school wasn't for me. We didn't make any immediate changes, and I toughed it out for a while, but I eventually abandoned Robert Morris for good. I never did cut my hair.

While all this was happening, the draft lottery was held. They didn't call my number so me and my 1A classification didn't have to go to Vietnam or to Canada after all.

I was still seeing my girlfriend at Cornell. I'd fly back and forth between Robert Morris in Pittsburgh to Ithaca, New York, home of Cornell University and the lovely Carol.

Carol, the girl who experienced Woodstock with me, was a headstrong individual. She was furiously protesting the war, fighting for women's liberation, and was against pretty much everything. I supported her causes for quite some time. We marched in Washington, DC. I got maced and was detained by the police once, but never arrested.

I also traveled to Chicago for some protests and met the people who eventually became known as the Chicago 7. I wasn't with them, or involved with inciting a riot, but I knew them, and they knew me.

At Cornell, Carol was friendly with some people who were very active in protesting the war. I got to know some of them too, on my visits. They were OK people, but I was shocked to find out they had built a little bomb factory.

I asked Carol about them, and she assured me they were just going to bomb some buildings, not people. I pointed out that, regardless of their focus on structures only, these guys were smoking weed, were wasted most of the time, and making bombs right below her apartment. It didn't bother her, but it was not the place I wanted to be. This is the point at which my relationship with Carol came to an end.

Still at a loss of what to do with my life, I majored in education and got a teaching certificate. I thought I would teach business law, marketing, and analytics to high school students. I liked teaching, but there wasn't much money in it. I never taught and eventually gave up on the idea of teaching as a profession. My education taught me how to teach and train, though. I've used these skills continuously in the print business and as a consultant, so I'm glad I did it.

My conflict about being against big business vs. the money that business provides still made things difficult for me. I was against business, but I wasn't against nice cars. I was driving a Jaguar XKE at the time — a vehicle that was entirely inconsistent with the anti-establishment person I thought I was.

Eventually I transferred to a school on Long Island – the New York Institute of Technology. By 1973, I was getting ready to graduate and resumed working part time for my father's print business. My job was on the collating line, which was all manual at the time. We walked around gathering sheets of paper and assembling them into a finished set.

By this time, ERS had about 30 AB Dick and Multilith presses, along with a couple of big Heidelberg offset presses. Dad looked around the city and saw all the businesses moving into large office buildings and predicted an increasing need for short-run duplicating. He worked with AB Dick and with Brunning Corporation, which made paper printing plates, to prepare for his vision of the printing evolution.

My father was an innovator and began experimenting with special inks that would work with the paper plates, combining technologies from multiple sources.

He converted the manual collation operation to in-line collators attached to the AB Dick machines. This allowed ERS to produce books and manuals, lowering the cost and increasing the speed. The knowledge he gained from this exploration of technology gave Hy Gimbel an advantage over his competitors.

By the early 1970s, my father felt the future of document reproduction was a technology called xerography. Xerography was invented by physicist Chester Carlson and later developed and commercialized by the Xerox Corporation. At the time, commercial application of xerography was rare, but Hy Gimbel foresaw the printing needs of businesses during this time and for decades to come. He started a new company, Xerographic Reproduction Center (XRC), and began a relationship with Xerox that has endured to this day through my company, Gimbel & Associates.

Bell Systems was a big client of my father's print company. He still had the ERS company, but also ran the XRC. They produced lots of reports and manuals for the Bell organization.

With my graduation from college, my father wanted to bring me into the business. He went to his partner and my uncle Harry insisted I start out at minimum wage. In 1973, this was about $1.60 an hour — not much for a recent college graduate. This is where I began working full time in the print business.

The more I worked with print, the better I liked it. Even though I wasn't making much money I'd already decided that a career in printing was going to pay better than teaching. I liked the printing business and enjoyed what I was learning about it. This was a big turning point for me. I finally had a vision of what I was going to be.

Though I had made the decision that printing was the place for me, I also knew that I didn't want to work for my dad forever. Though the business was still expanding, and Dad gave me the responsibility of starting up another site in New Jersey, I wasn't making the kind of money I wanted. I started thinking about getting into the copy business on my own.

The Itek Corporation had developed an innovative printing device called the Automatic Document System (ADS), which was a much more automated form of generating documents. The AB Dick and Multilith machines required lots of manual intervention. I thought the ADS might be a smart move for XRC and started investigating the equipment. In doing so, I became acquainted with Itek's sales manager, Dominic.

Dominic and I became friends. We started going out for drinks, partying at clubs, and having a good time. I told Dominic I wanted to open some copy centers, which turned out to be an interest we shared. We agreed to go into business together. We opened our first copy center at the corner of 7th Avenue and 23rd Street in New York. The site was a former Blimpie sub shop that had gone out of business.

Dominic had an investment in my business, but he was still working at Itek. He helped me acquire equipment as the business grew. Our second location was on 3rd Avenue.

It may sound like we had gotten down to serious business running the copy centers, and we were. But Dominic and I were also party people. We liked to have fun and somehow that interest turned into a discussion about why we should open our own discotheque.

We met with a man who owned a building in the city. He was a wealthy businessman, philanthropist, and heir to a family fortune. Somehow, Dominic and I convinced him that a disco was the perfect use for his building, and we opened our club called The Cork and Bottle.

To be completely honest, I think the motivation behind running a disco was so Dominic and I would have a place to party. It was probably not the best business decision I ever made. We never made any money at it. I can remember closing at the end of the night and asking Dominic if we had enough money left to pay the DJ. We'd both spend the evenings giving away drinks and being popular, so the cash receipts for the night could be underwhelming.

The lack of profits didn't seem important though. We had a good time, met a lot of people, and *we owned a club!* We had impressive reputations and a couple hundred people would show up at the club every night. We'd get home at 3:00 am and try to run the copy business the next day, after a night of drinking and dancing.

The next questionable move for Dominic and me was to open a clothing store. Neither of us knew anything about the clothing business, but we needed custom suits, so we'd look good at the clubs! This desire resulted in the unlikely decision to assume ownership of the Prince Sasha clothing store. We never made any money at that venture either, but boy, did we look good! I remember wearing some brilliant white suits with shirts open halfway to my navel. Hey, it was the '70s!

The club and the clothes made us almost celebrities. We got invited to great parties, went to Studio 54, ate in fancy restaurants, and met real celebrities like artist Peter Max and musician David Crosby.

We had no money, but we had the reputation. There was no place we'd go where people wouldn't know us. We felt important, even without strong financial backing.

I still had my long hair and I was leading a dual life. Part of the time I thought of myself as a partying college guy and the other part I was a serious businessman.

One thing important about this period is my partnership with Dominic. Even though we had crazy ideas, working with him showed me the value of making things happen. This would serve me well in later stages of my career. I've never been one to passively sit by and wait for opportunities to come my way, and I credit my business success partly to this approach.

Although we didn't know it at the time, our personal finances were about to improve. The timing couldn't be better as our business was growing, and we needed to open another facility.

The copy shops were leading us to corporate contracts that my partner and I would pursue aggressively. We were great talkers, Dominic and I, and we'd see company names on letterheads, get appointments with possible corporate clients, and then go and pitch them in person. This approach was very productive.

We weren't sophisticated financial investors, but Dominic had a friend giving him stock tips. He'd been told about a penny stock that looked especially attractive. The company was White Hall Drugs, trading on the stock exchange under the name Interstate Stores. The company was a small, two-store drug store chain operating under Chapter 10 of the US Bankruptcy code. The stock was selling for 75 cents.

Dominic, my father, and I gradually bought stock when we could scrape up the money, eventually ending up with about 5,000 shares each. Nothing was happening with the company, but according to the tipster, the company was poised to emerge from bankruptcy and expand operations. After several months of no activity, the stock price suddenly increased to a dollar. We were thrilled! Our investment had yielded us each about $1250 in profit.

In 1975 Dominic told me the company invited us to the stockholders' meeting. Apparently, we were major stockholders of this corporation! He thought we should buy some more stock. Since we'd closed the disco and the clothing store, and the printing business was making money, we had funds to invest. By the time of the stockholders' meeting, I held about 13,000 shares of this little drug store company stock.

Dominic and I drove all the way to company headquarters in Monticello, New York. We walked into the meeting to see a bunch of stodgy old men. I figured we were screwed. No way was this group going to pull off the drastic turnaround we'd anticipated.

The door opened and a man walked into the room carrying a huge stuffed giraffe and set it on the table. I knew then we'd probably lost every dollar we'd invested in this crazy company whose leader walks around the office with a stuffed animal under his arm.

The giraffe man said "Gentlemen, this is our new mascot. We're coming out of bankruptcy and we're opening new stores. But we won't be selling drugs anymore, we're switching to toys. The name of the stores will be Toys R Us."

I turned to Dominic and said, "We're dead. Who is going to walk into a toy store with such a goofy name and Geoffrey the Giraffe as the mascot?" It sounded ridiculous at the time. We left shortly thereafter.

Nothing happened with the stock for about two years. My dad lost interest and gave me his shares. My $18,000 investment was the most money I had at any one place. It was going nowhere, but I held onto it.

Years later, the stock finally started to increase in value. That 75-cent stock was trading at three dollars, then five dollars, but I still didn't sell.

After I got married, we wanted to buy a house in Roslyn, New York. We found a home that my wife Cheryl loved, and it was about a block away from my mother's house. The only money I had at the time was in the Toys R Us stock. The profits from sale of the stock would be enough to buy the house.

I called Murray, my stockbroker, and told him if the stock went up by another two dollars a share, to sell it. He tried to talk me out of it. Murray said I was making a mistake. He thought this stock was going to be a great investment and pleaded with me not to sell. Finally, I agreed to hold on to it until the price increased by another three dollars. At that point I would sell so I could buy the house we wanted.

Well, the stock did increase, the sale was made, and I bought the house.

For years, Murray would call me with updates on the stock that I no longer owned, just to let me know he was right about it. Over time it rose in price, split, rose again, split again. At its height, the stock, if I had held it, would have been valued at $57 million.

I should have kept half the stock. I still kick myself for that decision. But a lot of good came of it. Cheryl and I started our life together in that house, and our kids grew up there. That wouldn't have been possible without selling the Toys R Us stock when I did.

Since that time though, my investment strategy changed. I only buy now, I rarely sell. Missing out on millions of gains will do that to you.

I couldn't walk into a Toys R Us store for years. It was just too painful.

The company declared bankruptcy in 2017. They went through several years of tough times and eventually liquidated everything. In a final twist, the Gimbel Signage Group handled some of the signage for the liquidation sales.

* * *

In 1973 I was driving on the expressway and while stuck in a traffic jam, I ran out of gas. I wasn't alone. The Arab oil embargo caused a gasoline shortage in the United States. If you could buy gas at all, it was rationed. We waited in long lines at gas stations on designated days. People were stealing gas and endangering their lives by siphoning fuel from parked cars. Running out of gas wasn't an unusual occurrence.

Since I was stalled in the traffic jam, I left the car and climbed up an embankment to a diner where lots of other stranded motorists were waiting out the backup on the expressway. I got into a conversation with some people who recommended I take a trip to Acapulco. I guess I looked lonely, because they told me this Mexican vacation spot was a great place to meet women, which sounded good to me.

I took that trip along with my friend Miles. Our intent to meet women worked out great. I met Cheryl in Acapulco, and we married in 1979.

Who would think the Arabs would have such a big impact on my life? If I hadn't felt threatened by the anti-Semitic banners at college, I might never have changed schools. I could have chosen a different career and never got into the print business, never met Dominic, or bought stock in Toys R Us. And if the oil-producing Arab countries hadn't ceased exporting oil and caused a gas shortage, I'd never have met Cheryl and made a life and a family with her. It's funny how things turned out.

By now it's 1978. We're still running the copy stores, we'd built the new print factory, and things were going well. Then, in September something happened that would send my life in a drastically different direction.

2

. . .

1978 — 1983

Taking Over, and Union Threats

On September 8, 1978, I was working at the print company in Manhattan. It was about three o'clock on a Friday afternoon when my parent's housekeeper called and insisted I come home immediately. She was frantic. My brother-in-law Ronnie and I jumped in his Firebird and drove like maniacs. I ran red lights, passed cars on the expressway driving along the shoulder, and broke a bunch of traffic laws in my effort to get home as quickly as possible. I knew something had happened to my dad, and I knew it was bad.

If something was wrong with my father, the ambulance would take him to Deepdale Hospital, so that's where I went. I ran in yelling, "Hy

Gimbel! Where's Hy Gimbel!" When they told me he wasn't there, I knew the worst had happened.

My father's death at age 64 was totally unexpected. He was in good health and still full of the vigor he had as a young man. Just a couple of weeks before his death, he had an incident while driving with my mom in the car. Another driver cut them off and dad pulled in front of him, forcing the car to stop. My father got out of the car, pulled out his gun, and threatened the driver. "You won't endanger my wife that way," he said calmly. The guy called the cops who arrested dad and took his gun away. I got it back from the police after my father died.

The gun was for protection for when dad took money from the business to the bank. He had a carry permit and wore a holster. Dad was once held up by two men with guns that attacked him in the elevator as he was leaving work but couldn't get the gun out of the holster. Who knows what would have happened if he was successful?

No one messed with my dad. He grew up poor, getting his clothes at the Salvation Army and living in an apartment with fourteen people. His drive and entrepreneurial spirit made a comfortable life for us as I grew up, but my father was never much of a saver. All we had when he died was a small life insurance policy. Dad taught me the print business, so I guess that was part of his financial plan — for me to handle things if he could not. But when he died, we had some important financial decisions to make.

I still had my business with Dominic. We had three copy center stores and a production facility, separate from my father's business. My business life was important, but not what drove me. I was still the long-haired partier I'd been for the last nine years.

Mom was concerned about what we were going to do. "Don't worry," I told her, "Everything's going to be OK." My assurances were for mom's benefit. I had no idea what I should do. Suddenly, we had all these problems and issues, and it was up to me to handle things at the Xerographic Reproduction Center (XRC). I was only twenty-six years old.

Before he passed, my father was having conflicts with the union. He was trying to replace the union in his shop with another union. I knew little about what he was doing and nothing about any talks or negotiations that might have occurred.

About two years earlier, the union leaders, whom Dad characterized as racketeers, caused problems in the print shop over disagreements about pensions. To pressure my dad, the union encouraged Dad's employees to mishandle work, lose jobs, and purposely throw work away instead of delivering it to customers.

The union bosses met with Dad and assured him they could fix the "unrest" in the shop (which they themselves had encouraged). They asked for some "goodwill" compensation. It was a shakedown. Dad didn't put up with intimidation. That's why he was trying to change the union that represented his employees. After his death, I needed to pick up the pieces in this process but didn't know where to start.

We did put the business in my mother's name. Being a woman-owned business opened some doors to opportunities we wouldn't have had otherwise.

I wasn't entirely alone, but the ultimate responsibility for keeping Dad's company going fell on my shoulders. My uncle Phil was running operations, but he and many others were skeptical about my ability to step into my father's shoes and pull it off. They knew me as Roger the party guy; a young man who, in their eyes, was not serious about anything to do with business. They were taking bets about how badly I would screw it up.

I can see why the doubters worried about me. I'd led a wild and crazy lifestyle with motorcycles, fancy cars, discos, custom suits, and parties. But I'd also started and run a successful copy services business and made that shrewd investment in Toys R Us, which eventually allowed me to buy a very nice house for my family.

To make matters even more difficult as I transitioned to running my father's printing company, family disagreements between my father and his brother Harry had been brewing for about a year and a half. It started when Harry's son Richard graduated from college and wanted to work in the printing business. Uncle Harry wanted to pay Richard $25,000 a year.

Uncle Harry was the same guy who insisted that I start out at minimum wage as a college graduate. Now he wanted to pay my cousin much more. Dad thought it only fair to treat Richard the same as me, but Harry saw it differently and this disagreement broke up the partnership. Harry took the shop in New Jersey as his own business and my father kept everything else.

It wasn't long before the union took advantage of my father's passing. One day, I got a call from some union guys I didn't know very well. They said they'd been working on a deal with my father, and they wanted to meet me. I was instructed to meet them at a restaurant in Brooklyn on a Wednesday night. "Bring cash," they said, "we don't accept credit cards."

I drove to the place. This was in September, just a couple of days after we buried my father. Two guys wearing big heavy overcoats and hats met me at the door. It was still hot out, definitely not overcoat weather. I was pretty sure those overcoats were there to hide the weapons those men had on them.

The head union guy introduced me to his two associates, who never said a word the whole time I was there. They just nodded at me. Over dinner, the union man told me he'd been working a deal with my dad. I knew nothing of this deal that involved taking over representation of the workers in the shop. They said my father agreed to contract terms that would save the company about $250,000 a year. It was basically a done deal, he said. The only thing left was to finalize the transaction with a $50,000 cash "contribution" to the union leadership.

I didn't think the people who were currently representing the shop workers would ever agree to the terms these guys were quoting, and I told them so. He looked at me and said, "You don't understand. If we do this deal, you'll never hear from that union representative again. Bob and John here will never visit you either." I gulped. They were sort of subtle, but the message was clear. I was having dinner with a union racketeer and his two hit men.

I wanted to get out of there. I told them my dad just died and I needed to go home and figure some things out. They said "OK. Come back here on Friday."

I drove about four miles and had to pull over, I was shaking so much. I instinctively knew I couldn't mention this to anyone, and I didn't know what to do. We didn't have $50,000 in extra cash just lying around.

I withdrew my $10,000 in savings from the bank. The cash went into a paper bag, which I carried with me to the Friday meeting. I told them my father's estate was tied up in probate, which wasn't true. My uncle was fighting for control of the company, though, and I didn't know what was going to happen.

I handed over the paper bag full of money. "This is from me," I said. "It's all I have. I can't go through with the deal, but I know you guys did a lot of work on this and I want you to have this money. If something changes in the future I'll call you, but I just don't have access to the funds."

Even if I'd had the bribe money, I didn't want to do that deal. I knew I'd never be rid of them. They'd keep coming back, asking for more — forever.

I walked out of the meeting, leaving the $10,000 behind, and thankfully, never heard from them again.

To this day, I do not know if my father really negotiated that union deal or if it was all made up. I eventually re-negotiated my labor contract with the existing union by threatening to close the business if I didn't get the concessions I needed to keep the business alive. My reputation as a party guy actually helped in this case. The union thought I might just be crazy enough to shutter the company, and they agreed to terms more favorable to me.

Not long after this event I had another encounter with people who specialized in intimidation to get what they wanted.

One of our large accounts for the business I took over when my dad died was retailer JCPenney. We dealt with a couple of print buyers there. Both happened to be named John. To keep them straight, I always referred to them as John and Little John.

Little John came from an Italian family, and he liked to fish. We'd taken him out on the boat several times and became friends. One day, in the spring of 1979, he asked me if I would take some of his friends out fishing. He said they didn't like to go out a lot, but he knew they'd really enjoy the boat if he was with them.

The friends lived in Brooklyn, and Little John asked if I'd pick them up at Freeport. I said OK. We scheduled the day, and I reminded Little John to tell his friends they had to dress appropriately for being on the boat. It seemed these people were probably not experienced sailors, and I wanted to make sure they would be safe.

I arrived at Freeport and saw six guys wearing black suits and shiny shoes. They were carrying a big vat of homemade tomato sauce and pasta. They wanted to heat it up and eat on the boat. I was a little concerned about this group, but Little John introduced us and we headed out to go fishing.

It was a little rough on the water that day. I made anyone up on the deck take off their shiny shoes so they didn't slide off the boat. They took off their jackets, caught some fish, and proceeded to have a good time. Two of the men were down in the galley, cooking up the pasta.

I heard a crash from below and went down to see tomato sauce everywhere. We cleaned it up as much as possible, even off the ceiling, but the white shag carpeting was a goner. They apologized, but I told them not to worry about it. What was I going to do? These were friends of an important person at a big customer; it wouldn't do to get upset.

We were out all day, and the trip was a success. John's friends were older Italian gentlemen, and they were thrilled at their experience. I could tell that one of them was an important guy. His name was Carmine.

When we returned to the dock, Carmine thanked me. He told me he was having a big party in Brooklyn and wanted me to come. Cheryl and I would be his special invited guests and we would sit on the dais with Carmine and his wife. I looked over at Little John and he was mouthing the word "go". I got the message that it would be unwise to turn down this invitation, and I accepted.

They held the party in a big event hall. There must have been 300-400 people there. My wife and I were seated on the dais, and I watched as people came up to Carmine to kiss his hand. I didn't know who he was, but I clearly had underestimated his importance in the Italian community.

The man's name was Carmine Galante, nicknamed "The Cigar" and "Lilo" (a Sicilian word for cigar) because of his fondness for cigars. He was very nice to us and introduced my wife and me to all his friends and associates at this party.

I still didn't know who he was, so I pulled Little John aside.

"Who is this guy?" I asked John.

"Carmine is the head of the Bonanno family," he informed me.

Now he tells me! The Bonanno family was one of the "Five Families" that ran organized crime in New York and across the US. They were known as one of the most brutal of the criminal organizations known as the American Mafia. The family was famously infiltrated by an undercover FBI agent calling himself Donnie Brasco, which of course no one knew about at the time. I never figured out how Galante was connected to Little John and I didn't really want to know.

I gulped as "The Cigar" handed me a cigar and invited me to smoke with him in the parking lot.

The funny thing was, he was a nice guy if you ignored the part about being a ruthless hit man suspected of being involved in over eighty murders. When he asked if he could go fishing again, I suggested he call me in the summer. This, I thought, was the most appropriate response at the time, given the circumstances. We parted cordially.

A couple of months later, the newspapers reported three men wearing ski masks killed Carmine Galante while he and some associates lunched at an Italian restaurant in Brooklyn. He died with a cigar in his mouth.

When the news of Galante's death broke, I called my attorney. I'd had this guy on my boat just a few weeks ago. Would the authorities think I was involved in his criminal activities? Should I be worried?

The attorney assured me that the FBI had probably had Galante under surveillance for a long time. They already knew about the fishing trip and understood I wasn't part of an organized crime family's lawlessness. Still, for about a month, I worried about having to explain myself to the authorities.

What if someone had tried to kill "The Cigar" while he was on my boat? Spilled tomato sauce would be the least of my problems.

As unprepared as I was, I was fortunate to take over the business on the cusp of an economic boom. In the late '70s and into the '80s, if a business was operational, it was making money. That included the printing business, where demand for short run print had exploded. If you weren't a dummy in the 1980s, you were going to make money.

Technology was exploding at this time. New developments in xerographic printing devices were just around the corner and I was going to be involved.

3

. . .

1982

A Really Big Project

In 1982, the government ordered XRC's biggest customer, AT&T, to divest their company. I was home one night when the phone rang at one o'clock in the morning. My wife and I had just returned from a Saturday night out. Unexpectedly, I was on the phone talking to a group of AT&T executives who were all in a conference room somewhere using a rudimentary speaker phone the company had developed. The technology was crude by today's video teleconferencing standards, but it was brand new back then.

The ringing phone had woken one of my kids who was crying, and I'd been drinking a good part of the night. It wasn't the best time to be talking to the CFO of a huge multi-national company, along with AT&T's CEO and the rest of the board of directors. I went to the kitchen to pick up the extension phone.

The CFO told me they were divesting their regional operating companies. At the time, XRC was supplying AT&T with large volumes of documentation related to their monopoly cases with the US government, along with other documents. They called me because they had a high-priority project. "OK," I said, "What do you need?"

"We have about 500,000 pages of documents. We need 10,000 copies of them."

I was sure I had mis-heard him. Maybe the static-laden speakerphone had muddled his words. "Would you repeat that?" I asked.

"We need 10,000 copies made of 500,000 original contracts. Since we already do business with you, we wanted to see if you could do this job for us," said the man on the phone.

I asked him to hold on. AT&T was our biggest customer. Losing them would put us out of business. Answering "no" wasn't an option, but I needed to think carefully about how I was going to answer "yes". I grabbed a calculator and tried to clear my head.

Something didn't look right with this job, besides the fact that it was a completely unreasonable request. They wanted to start printing this job in six hours — at 7:00 am Sunday morning – and complete it in three or four days. I didn't think there was enough paper in the entire tri-state area to print this job.

I told the CFO I ran the two biggest printing plants in the city, and I would begin printing everything they could send me by opening both plants in the morning.

I guess these executives didn't know how to use the speaker phone because they didn't mute it while they talked among themselves. I heard them discussing their options. They eventually decided that dealing with us was their only viable solution and came back on the line, wanting a price quote.

I started scribbling numbers on a notepad, trying to figure out how much to charge for a rush job that included overtime labor, rush shipments on paper, and handling for a boxcar full of documents. If I underpriced it, the loss on a job this size would be devastating. On the other hand, I knew they were desperate; they called me at one in the morning! But I didn't want to price it too high and lose this job to someone else, especially when AT&T had just told me the company was splitting up. I might lose the account for good. Should I tell them $60,000? $80,000?

I'd been drinking. I should haven't been doing spur-of-the-moment critical math calculations on a notepad, but I had no choice. The entire executive team of one of the world's largest companies was waiting for my answer. The baby was crying, my wife was looking at me with concern, and I was freaking out.

The CFO bailed me out. "Mr. Gimbel," he said, "Can you bring this in for a million dollars?"

I swallowed hard and told him that yes, I'd do it for a million dollars. My wife had just picked up an extension phone and heard my answer. The CFO and I exchanged contact information, I promised to be in the shop by five in the morning to get started, and we ended the call.

"What just happened?" I asked my wife.

"I don't know, but they agreed to pay you a million dollars for something," she said.

Into the city I went, calling in all my people at the plants and getting ready for this onslaught of work. As it turned out, the job wasn't 10,000 copies all at once. We received 500,000 originals though, printed a variable number of copies of each document, and sent them to attorneys. The lawyers marked them up with revisions and returned them to us to print new versions. It was still a huge job, but not as intimidating as it first appeared. Still, we set up cots in the shop and slept there during this high-pressure job where access to the area was restricted due to the sensitive nature of the documents.

We ended up printing the actual contracts that went to the split-off entities for signature. I think it's awesome that we printed the divestiture of AT&T, for which the company paid us 1 million dollars.

I won't tell you how much profit we made on this job, but I promise you it was a very healthy margin. We got paid a lot because we could deliver what the customer wanted, do the work accurately, respond rapidly, and deliver on time. These are all keys to business success I learned from my father, Hy Gimbel.

Of course, when AT&T broke up, our contract with the parent company was transferred to all the new companies. Because we'd done all this work at the very beginning, all the new entities already knew us and we became the print supplier for all of them. Added together, this work ended up being greater than what we'd been doing for AT&T before the break-up. Because we now had seven customers instead of one, we could accept more work from each and our AT&T business exploded.

Many years later, I was at a party when a man tapped me on the shoulder. "Do you remember me?" he asked. I didn't.

"I was the CFO on the call that night you took on the AT&T divestiture print job many years ago. Let me buy you a drink."

We sat at the bar and he said, "I'm going to tell you something, but you can't hold me to it."

"Remember that night on the phone? When we hung up, all the executives were shaking my hand for negotiating that deal with you. They were willing to spend $10 million to do that job, so they were overjoyed at the arrangement we made."

I was shocked. But I told him the job wasn't worth $10 million. I did the right job at the right price at the right time, and I got paid satisfactorily for that work. I appreciated the relationship with AT&T, and I would have taken advantage of them by charging more. That's not the way I work.

Then I went home, kicking myself in the butt a little.

But really, my decision at the time of the AT&T job and the conversation with the CFO years later fit a pattern that has served me well over the years. I'm always setting the stage for the next step. In this case, it certainly paid off with additional profits and a long-term relationship with a valuable customer.

The AT&T divestiture project led to other work for XRC. It also created a new entity and I found myself working with them as well — a profitable relationship that lasted much longer than I'd ever imagined.

4

. . .

1983

DocuTech and XPODS

A round this time, I developed a relationship with Xerox, who was coming out with some new equipment I thought would change the printing world. The latest equipment, code-named the Zenith, was ultimately released as the DocuTech. I wanted to replace all the older AB Dick equipment in my shops, and it looked like Xerox's new technology would be a game-changer. We were alpha testers for the DocuTech, allowing us to see the benefits of the technology before it was even on the market, and we furnished Xerox with valuable testing data and feedback.

In the mid-80s we were cranking out huge volumes of pages for clients like AT&T and JCPenney. Xerox wanted us to test the DocuTech machines so they could see how their equipment performed under such loads.

The original design created high volume copies by scanning pages and storing the images before printing. We wondered if we could send files directly to the device and skip the scanning function. The approach sounds obvious today, but back then it was impossible to connect the DocuTech to a data source. Xerox was using a proprietary file format called DocuBlob, a sort of random bitmap arrangement. No outside software existed that could generate DocuBlob files. We started working with Xerox on this idea of sending printable files to the DocuTech.

Xerox had flown me and a handful of corporate executives to Dallas to film us talking about the still-unveiled DocuTech for advertising purposes. The executives had never seen the machine, but these corporate leaders would talk about what they wanted to see in new print technology. I was there to talk about what the machine could do.

After the filming and dinner, all the executives left. Xerox's head technology engineer for DocuTech and I were the only ones remaining, and I convinced him we should commandeer the limo and go see some sights. I'd never been to Dallas, and I wanted to check out the local scene. We ended up going to a bunch of clubs around town. I, of course, was comfortable in that environment as a place to have fun, but also to do business. I took the opportunity at one club to talk to the engineer about connecting DocuTechs to the outside world so we could transfer and control the information going to the machine. He told me Xerox was working on a solution, but it wasn't developed yet.

I explained to him that the line to connect the DocuTech wasn't the only problem. We needed to communicate job parameters to the machine in the form of electronic job tickets and get feedback from the equipment. For each job, I needed to know how many copies, what paper to use, finishing requirements, and other details about the jobs. That way, the DocuTech could enable its many functions automatically.

The man from Xerox and I got some paper and started listing all the functionality I thought would make the DocuTech a better device. When we finished, he agreed it was a terrific list. But he said Xerox wouldn't build it. He suggested I do it because I understood all the needs so well. Of course, I'm a printer, not a programmer. I couldn't create this front-end processing system we'd envisioned.

The engineer understood, and he gave me a name — Denise at NEPS in Nashua, New Hampshire. Back then, I'd never heard of NEPS or Denise. He assured me that NEPS could do what was necessary to create the functionality he and I had listed on the paper while clubbing in Dallas.

The following week, I drove to Nashua to meet with Denise. I couldn't tell her about the DocuTech; it was still a secret. But I pulled out my list and told her I needed a front end that could do all those things. She read through the list and told me she could do it.

One of the stumbling blocks to automation and productivity was the speed at which the DocuTech could accept data. It was limited to 30-40 pages per minute. Denise said I needed to talk to Joel at Xerox. According to Denise, Joel was working on a secret project that would solve the problem. It turned out Joel was leading a small group of engineers working on powering the DocuTech with a Sun Microsystems computer. When the integration was complete, Xerox doubled the data transmission speed.

It was crazy. Here we were, putting together a business deal based on technology nobody could talk about! Denise suggested a partnership, which sounded like a good idea. I came up with a name for the yet-to-be created front end: XPODS — Xerographic Print on Demand System. I designed the system and Denise built it.

Joel's team had boosted the DocuTech's data transfer speed by changing the operating platform from a PC to a Sun Microsystems Solei.9 processor. It still wasn't quite fast enough, so we tweaked XPODS. We pre-RIP'ed the files and stored them, allowing us to run the printer as fast as it could go. We could stack up the jobs and then run them. Productivity was 30% better than any other digital printing device.

With the help of William Martin, we sold XPODS to several print service operations. William had been in the audience when I was giving a presentation and said he wanted to work for me. I hired him to help run the XPODS business.

William is still with me all these years later. He eventually took an executive leadership position at Gimbel & Associates.

Xerox eventually made their own version of our XPODS product, which was in large part a copy of what the NEPS/Gimbel partnership invented. They called this product XDODS — Xerox Documents on Demand System — even the name was almost the same as ours! This product evolved and became DigiPath, and then eventually FreeFlow, which is now the Xerox front end product. FreeFlow still contains much of the original designs that I created for XPODS years ago.

Years later, I was at a party and was approached by a Xerox employee I'd known for some time. She bought me a drink and told me she'd deny ever telling me, but that Xerox could never have developed their XDODS/DigiPath/FreeFlow product had it not been for the design I created for XPODS. Xerox knew they needed the product but wouldn't have thought of half the functions we built into XPODS.

XPODS and DocuTechs played a part in XRC's next big deal and our venture into a new way of providing service. Again, the break-up of AT&T was the spark that set us in a new direction.

5

. . .

1984 — 1993

Bellcore and Xerox

The breakup of AT&T created some new companies and XRC had contracts to supply printing services to all of them. One of the new companies was Bell Communications Research, or Bellcore. Bellcore was established as a central command and data collection entity for the seven regional phone companies that were formerly part of AT&T — the "Baby Bells".

Bellcore provided needed consistency in documentation and workflow so the companies could handle phone calls identically, regardless of where calls originated throughout the country. Bellcore oversaw software, infrastructure, transitions, formats, and functionality. The

Baby Bells had to follow thousands of standard operating procedures (SOPs) as dictated by the divesture agreement with the federal government. Bellcore enabled this compliance.

Bellcore occupied twelve buildings in New Jersey, and they needed printing services, so they issued a request for quote (RFQ). Our company was, of course, included in the RFQ distribution. We probably knew more about the printing needs of this organization than they did themselves. Xerox Corporation was also bidding on the Bellcore contract.

When Bellcore issued their RFQ for the printing services as a facilities management contract, we initially began working with Xerox on our response. I knew if we won the contract that we'd be needing lots of new Xerox equipment, so it made sense to work together — until I figured out they were going to bid against us!

Around this time, Xerox created several advisory councils with members chosen from Xerox's largest customers. Each council focused on an aspect of the printing industry, such as commercial print, digital print, and small copier. One set of councils concentrated on the US market and another separate set of councils focused on Europe.

Xerox invited me to sit on the commercial print council where I met the head of production, IT, and logistics at Xerox.

He and I had several adversarial conversations about Xerox's new Document Technology Centers (DTCs) that offered printing services to clients. The DTC centers were competing with me and other commercial printers, and I didn't think it was right. They sold me equipment and then turned around and tried to sign up customers I was planning on servicing with the gear I'd just bought!

The Bellcore RFQ was an example of the unfairness of the DTCs. I was putting together a proposal that would include the purchase of a lot of Xerox equipment to produce Bellcore's work, and Xerox was preparing their own response, featuring the DTCs! The DTCs could get their Xerox hardware at a much lower cost than anyone else. This gave them an unfair advantage.

I was leading the charge to object to Xerox's business practice, but the entire commercial print advisory council was with me. We argued and complained, but we weren't getting anywhere. Meanwhile, XRC had to respond to the Bellcore RFQ, and we came up with a plan.

By converting a single Bellcore warehouse into a centralized print production facility, we could drastically reduce the amount of equipment necessary to serve the needs at Bellcore. Each of the buildings would house a small reprographics center, but we would do all the high-volume production in the central facility.

This hub and spoke approach to document production required less equipment, which not only lowered costs by about 1 million dollars a year, but it also reduced Xerox's competitive advantage.

The innovative hub and spoke plan for Bellcore print fulfillment wasn't new to XRC. We'd been using the same concept with our Manhattan retail stores. But no one had ever tried something like this in a facilities management environment.

Further expanding the hub and spoke solution, we proposed to transport any overflow work, or work requiring specialized equipment like web presses, to our New York production centers.

After we submitted our proposal, I got a call from an official at Bellcore. He wanted me to come to New Jersey and talk about the proposal. He challenged the idea that our solution would save Bellcore a million dollars a year. "What makes you 100% sure?" he asked.

"I'm so confident we can save you that money, I'll guarantee it in writing," I responded. "But," I continued, "You must guarantee me a minimum number of impressions. Plus, if you cancel the contract, you agree to pay off the leases for all the machinery."

Liquidated damages were important because the contract on which we were bidding included a sixty-day cancellation clause. If Xerox won the bid and Bellcore cancelled the contract, Xerox could just take their equipment back and sell it to someone else. If we won, I didn't have that luxury. I'd be stuck with the Xerox hardware and no work to support it. A liquidated damage clause would force Bellcore to buy the equipment from me if they cancelled the contract.

Bellcore wanted assurances we could do what we proposed, and I referred him to all our New York accounts. I pointed out that Bellcore would recover space in all their buildings and make use of the warehouse that was currently empty.

I planned to staff the Bellcore operation with about thirty of my employees already familiar with the hub and spoke arrangement and to use productivity enhancing technology like Xerox DocuTechs and the XPODS system. We'd supply the trucks and drivers to pick up and deliver the work and eventually also picked up their outbound mail as well. I was eager to win this bid that would double the size of our business and I knew we'd be able to deliver the promised cost savings to our customer.

We eventually negotiated lengthening the contract to five years instead of three, with liquidated damages. Bellcore awarded us the contract.

Even with the assurances I'd secured from Bellcore, the project presented some risks. At the end of the five-year agreement, we would face large balloon payments for all that equipment we'd gotten from Xerox. Even before we won the contract, I was banking on extensions that would help pay for the equipment.

In the end, the contract was extended three times. We were at Bellcore for fifteen years and made millions of dollars doing that contracted work, plus other projects, as we became the sole provider of print services for the entire organization. This was a big deal. Most mid-size printers did not have contracts that guaranteed them work over long time periods. Nobody had contracts and guaranteed volumes worth $15 million.

The Bellcore deal was XRC's first facilities management engagement and raised our annual revenue by over 30%. By the mid-1980s, we were running print operations at twelve of our customers' sites in a facilities management role.

We moved the DocuTech, which was still code-named Zenith and a closely guarded secret, to a secure room at the Bellcore document factory. Very few people were allowed to even see the machine. We also added the XPODS system to boost performance — the first commercial installation for the system we built in partnership with NEPS.

Xerox eventually agreed with the commercial print council's stand on the Xerox DTC centers and closed most of them. Three remaining DTCs serviced existing contracts, but Xerox stopped competing directly with their own customers. I admired my Xerox adversary for stepping up to do the right thing and we developed a friendship that lasted for years.

My relationship with Xerox was complicated. Sometimes I was a customer, sometimes a partner, and sometimes a competitor. This made it difficult at times, but the company was developing printing hardware and software I knew would be important for my business and the printing industry. I did my best to maintain a balanced and mutually beneficial relationship.

After my father passed away, I inherited his boat, the Lady Audrey Three, named after my mother. By 1983, I was still learning how to use this 53-foot vessel. Interestingly, this boat was originally owned by Oscar-winning actress Susan Hayward. You can see a picture of this boat on the picture page at the front of this book.

The boat was a way to entertain our customers. We'd take them out on day cruises, go fishing, participate in shark tournaments at Montauk, New York, and have a great time all summer. I loved relaxing with our customers in this way. I didn't have a disco anymore, but the boat was a good substitute. I met a lot of great boating people during this time and boating is still something that I enjoy whenever I can find time to get away.

We had a boat captain in 1983, Bob. He was an old salt who used to go to the bars and tell stories of all his adventures. I can remember him always wearing his captain's hat, an unbuttoned short-sleeved shirt, and a shark tooth hanging around his neck. Captain Bob was quite the character. He stayed on after Dad died to help me with the boat.

In September of '83, I decided I wanted to sail the boat from New York, where it was berthed, all the way to Florida. A good friend from AT&T, Captain Bob, and I were the crew. We had a fourth crewmember lined up, a young man who had worked for me for three years. But the day we were to sail, he disappeared. No one ever heard from him again. I still don't know what happened to the man.

We were almost to Florida when we pulled into an area called Pablo Creek in South Georgia, where the government was building a submarine base. We didn't know it, but a dredging crew had dumped all the silt into the channel and we ran aground while traveling at 16 knots (about 20 mph). The impact did a lot of damage. We had no electricity, the radios weren't working, and no one was around.

We were stuck sideways on the sand bar until we dug out behind the boat and backed it out. Unfortunately, we hit a hidden underwater wall, broke the rudders, and ran over the obstruction with the props. Once we were free, we managed to use the engine throttles to steer the boat and limped our way to a marina sixty miles away, where we pulled in for repairs. Good thing we had an experienced captain on board!

Captain Bob stayed with the boat while it was out of the water and new rudders were built and installed. The rest of us flew home.

Eventually, we got the boat to Florida where we rented a slip to store the boat. I made a deal with the Marriott Harbor Beach resort. My family joined the cabana club, and we enjoyed the hotel facilities during the day and slept with the kids on the boat at night. This was our family vacation spot for almost ten years. My fishing buddies would also fly with me down to Florida where we'd fish on Thursday, Friday, and Saturday. Everyone would fly home on Sunday afternoon.

The boat was part of both my family life and the business world. It still is.

OK, back to business! From 1983 through the early nineties, we built our own business and sold about eight of the XPODS systems to other printing companies. An investor from San Francisco, bought NEPS during this time also, around 1988. Since we were partners with NEPS, I met with the investor. He wanted to buy NEPS to resell it. I told him he'd have to buy out my interest in XPODS as part of the deal, which he did.

Since Xerox was coming out with their own solution, I felt the opportunity to sell more XPODS was ending. Xerox would be a strong competitor, which would make it more difficult for my company to sell more systems. I didn't feel too bad about giving up XPODS, but as part of the deal I was allowed to keep the three systems I had running in my own shops. We kept acquiring DocuTechs, having about twelve of them installed at one point, and used XPODS to continue to hold a productivity advantage over most of our competitors.

Though we were no longer partners, I remained friends with Denise and her team, and still am. NEPS still sells a version of the XPODS system called NDemand.

What eventually became the International Printers' Network (IPN) started in the same era as the Bellcore deal and I was privileged to be involved in the formation of this group. I didn't know it at the time, but the IPN and international travel were to become an important factor in what would become my second career.

6

. . .

Going International

In 1990, Xerox brought the North American and European councils together for an event in Spain. I met people from all over the world who were doing the same kind of work as XRC, using the same equipment. Eventually, we started talking about working together in some way. We convinced Xerox to hold the next council meeting as a joint affair so we could work out a cooperative arrangement.

At this joint meeting, we formed the International Printers Network (IPN). Through this organization, the members could send print jobs to partners for production and distribution almost anywhere in the world. It was a globally distributed printing solution!

Xerox continued to play a part in IPN for many years — the members were all Xerox customers, so it was in the company's best interest to facilitate the organization. Eventually, we decided to break from Xerox and the organization has operated independently ever since. I was the second chairman of IPN and served for ten years. I'm still involved with IPN as a board member and Director of Sponsorship.

The IPN group took distributed printing a step further in working with a newspaper company called Presspoint. Presspoint took news stories from newspapers across the world, printed selected stories and excerpts, and distributed their own newspaper in the United States. My company, XRC, received files from 26 to 30 global newspapers at 4:00 in the afternoon. We printed the articles on the DocuTechs, bound the pages, and delivered them to JFK Airport and Newark Airport in time for them to be handed out to travelers on Virgin Airlines flights beginning at 8:00 PM. The banner at the top of page one said "Blimey! Our planes must be faster than we thought. You're reading tomorrow's news today!" This was true. The original newspapers in Europe were not yet on the streets by the time we finished publishing the Presspoint newspapers in the US.

We still use the distributed print model today. Gimbel & Associates helped a customer develop a system to compose print in New York destined for delivery to the Midwest. They transmit the files to their facility in California and print it in time to hand the finished product over to FedEx for overnight delivery to Ohio. We enabled our customer to satisfy their needs by taking advantage of the time zones.

IPN allowed me to travel to many countries to talk about printing and train people. I became a spokesman for the industry.

One time, I was asked to speak in Japan. The room held about 500 men in one room and 300 women in another hall. In Japan, they separated the sexes back then. All the attendees were listening to translators on headsets. I didn't speak Japanese, and I was concerned about the translation. Would the translators be able to follow me? Would their words make sense to the audience? This was my biggest audience ever, and I was the keynote. I really wanted things to go over well.

Before my talk, I met with the translators. My presentation included some technical details, and I wanted to make sure they understood. I also wanted to tell a joke to loosen up the audience.

"No, no," said the translators, "No joke in Japan!"

This was important to me. I wanted the crowd to like me and listen to the rest of the presentation, so I told the translators I'd explain the joke to them. They looked skeptical but agreed.

We went over the joke a few times and I thought the translators understood it. After a couple of hours of going through the slides, we were prepared.

Later, when I started my presentation and got to the joke, everyone laughed. I was thrilled! I had the audience in my hand, and they were into me! The rest of the presentation went well, and I got lots of applause when I finished.

At the reception following my talk, I went to thank the translators. "I have to ask you," I said, "It seemed that you shortened my joke." It was sequential translation, so I would say my part, wait for the translation, and then continue, so I knew the joke translation didn't sound quite right.

The translators looked at each other and then told me, "We didn't really understand your joke, so we just said 'The American said something funny. Please laugh.'"

Here I thought I was a big hit as a comedian, and they never even heard the joke!

A companion in my travels around the world was my son, Hunter. When he was in his twenties, he helped me set up and run the events. We visited 25 cities and always arrived a day early or stayed a day later to experience different cultures and see the sights. It was a bonding experience neither of us will ever forget. We even went on safari in Kruger Park in South Africa.

In 2005, Hunter and I boarded a flight on South African Air from New York to Johannesburg, where we were doing another presentation. I'd already booked the safari, but first we had to store our safari gear and then fly to Capetown for the event. Overall, it took us twenty-seven hours — our longest trip ever.

After a successful event, we returned to Johannesburg. My son and I packed all our posters and other presentation materials and headed to a small airport where we'd take a single-engine prop plane to our safari lodge. We changed in the bathroom and waited in the hangar along with four other tourists.

I'd never traveled on a small plane, so it made me a bit nervous. I don't like heights, and the feel in a small aircraft made me more conscious of being up in the air.

The trip was fine, however. Though the plane was small, we all did well as the pilot and co-pilot passed back sandwiches for us to eat along the way. Two hours later, we began our approach to land at Kruger Park.

The weather was cloudy, so the pilot explained they'd have to land using instruments since they couldn't see the ground.

The "instrument" was a single tower. We'd fly in spirals around the tower until we got to the ground. Hunter and I, along with our fellow passengers, all had concerned looks on our faces about this maneuver. We couldn't see anything as we flew through the clouds.

Eventually, we broke through the clouds and landed on a dirt runway in the middle of the South African brush. The only visible structure for miles was a tiny building, which was unoccupied. Our pilot unloaded our gear, Hunter and I got off the plane, and he took off. The other passengers were going somewhere else.

Here we were in the middle of nowhere, all by ourselves!

It wasn't long though, until a Range Rover appeared. It had an open roof and four men with rifles. We loaded up, and I asked how far it was to the lodge. I could see no evidence of human occupation.

"We'll be there in about two and a half hours," the driver replied.

What a trip! Two hours on a little plane and another two and a half hours riding in a Range Rover with gun-toting guides before we would even get to the facility.

Jock Lodge was a beautiful place once we got there, and our trip started to feel more like a vacation and less like a tortuous journey to nowhere, 35 hours from civilization in New York. We walked by the helicopter parked outside and proceeded to an orientation session.

At the orientation, all the tourists were cautioned about the dangers of the South African brush country. They assured us if we followed the rules, everyone would be fine. We were not to leave the Range Rover unless a ranger said it was OK, and we should refrain from touching things. Sounded reasonable to me.

Then they told us about the snakes — particularly the black mamba snakes. Black mambas are highly venomous. They can grow to a length of over nine feet and travel at a top speed of nearly ten miles per hour.

"If you get bit by a black mamba," said the lodge official, "we have to put you on the helicopter and take you to a hospital in Johannesburg."

I asked why they didn't have anti-venom at the lodge. They explained that if the bite didn't break the skin and they gave us the anti-venom, it would kill us.

At this point, I began to wonder why I thought this safari was a good idea. Hunter was fine. He was taking pictures and was excited to be there. His dad, not so much.

Leaving the orientation, the first thing I saw was a snake crossing the pathway. It wasn't a black mamba, but it did nothing to raise my comfort level at the time.

We got to our room, and I made sure to shake out the sheets, just to make sure we weren't sharing our accommodations with any snakes or other inhabitants of the wild country.

We did our first safari ride that first evening, just as it was getting dark. It was a three-hour excursion. Six guests and two rangers headed off into the gathering darkness.

According to the brochure from the safari company, each safari should treat their guests to a view of what they called the "Big 5" animals in Kruger Park — elephant, buffalo, leopard, lion, and rhino. On that first venture out into the brush, we could get out of the Range Rovers and walk around some. The night noises were incredible. We saw some hyenas.

The next day, they woke us at 6:00 am for a morning ride into the wilderness, with breakfast when we returned. The official schedule called for guests to relax around the pools at the lodge until it was time for another guided tour in the evening.

I didn't mind relaxing for a couple of hours, but it seemed wasteful to have come all that way and do nothing all day. It was hot, but I'd rather be out seeing some things. I negotiated with the staff and all the guests in our group chipped in with some money, which got us extra African safari activities each day. On one of these trips, we got to watch lions bathing in the river. It was very cool.

The lodge was occupied by a large number of small, very friendly monkeys. They'd hop around in the trees above us while guests used the outdoor showers and we had fun playing with them.

The trip was fantastic. Now I'm glad we did it. Hunter took tons of pictures, and we really enjoyed the experience. My favorite was a cougar that came up to the vehicle. It was the most beautiful animal I'd ever seen, and it was right up close. One thing I learned is that cougars can run very fast to catch their prey, but they tire and have trouble fighting off the opportunistic hyenas that come and take the kill from the cougars.

Hunter and I had great bonding experiences in our travels for about five years, but one day he came to me and told me he wanted to work with people his own age. All the print company owners were older, and he didn't feel he could teach them anything. My son wanted to work in finance.

Today, Hunter is married to Samantha and has three kids. He runs his own financial services company. Though I'd told him all those years ago he'd always have a job with me if he wanted to come back, he's made the life he wanted for himself — just like his old man.

In another international experience, I developed a program for Xerox called Digitally Cool. When I presented, I came onstage in a full snowsuit, carrying a snowboard. The audience had just watched a video featuring an extreme snowboarder, and I was wearing the same suit as the professional snowboarder in the video. I'd come out and say, "This is cool — digitally cool! We're going to show you stuff that's cooler than that!" Then I'd go offstage, change out of the snowsuit and return wearing the business suit I had underneath.

Usually, this worked great. We'd done this bit in about twenty cities. In India, we didn't do so well. They'd never seen snow, and when I peeled off the snowsuit, it looked like I'd been swimming in my business clothes, it was so hot.

Also representing Xerox, I was traveling with Randy, who years later ended up working for me at Gimbel & Associates. At the time, he worked for Xerox. During one trip through South America, we had an engagement in Venezuela.

One night, Randy had a dinner engagement elsewhere, and I remained at the hotel to eat at the hotel's very nice restaurant. I walked into the fancy restaurant and sat down. Shortly, I noticed military guards in full bomb suits standing by the door, along with other armed soldiers. I didn't know what was going on until Hugo Chavez, the president of Venezuela, came in and sat down. Chavez and I were the only diners in the restaurant. The soldiers blocked anyone else from entering. I guess I got in just before the lockdown.

At first, I didn't know who my fellow diner was, so I asked the waiter and he informed me I was sitting across the room from the powerful president of the country. I wanted to say hello, but the server warned me not to approach the man. Given the level of security and the weapons in the room, that was probably good advice. I waved and Chavez waved back.

Randy returned from his dinner, impressed that I'd "had dinner" with Hugo Chavez!

All these international travel experiences, the speaking, and the relationships through IPN have influenced me as a person and a businessman. I've been able to see how print is done in many other countries and how it fits into different societies. This has given me a perspective of my industry that I couldn't have had any other way. I even went supersonic, flying to Paris on the Concorde in 1999. I've met lots of great, interesting people that have made for a fulfilling life.

7

. . .

High School, Motorcycles, and Jamaican Adventures

I grew up in Roslyn, New York, a colorful New England type of town on Long Island. It was a great place to live, but my town had its share of head shops and drugs were readily available. It also had some great concert venues like My Father's Place, Heads & Tails, and US Blues. Many famous artists performed in these small places including Bob Weir from the Grateful Dead, George Carlin, Madonna, Bruce Springsteen, and Richie Havens.

Roslyn was also home to a restaurant called George Washington Manor, so named because our first president had visited there in 1790. My father always had a desire to buy the restaurant, but mom put her foot down, saying she wasn't going to be married to a restaurateur!

Living in Roslyn, New York, I had a bunch of friends, including my pals Robert and Alan. The three of us developed a reputation as outcasts in our early teens because of how we operated. As kids, we were always up to something to which our parents would probably disapprove, so we didn't tell them. Alan had access to his parents' liquor cabinet. Like a million other kids sneaking their parents' booze, we disguised what we drank by adding water to the bottles. I don't know if Alan's parents ever caught on.

At thirteen years old, Alan would take his dad's car and drive us into the city. Alan wasn't a tall kid. He sat on a phone book so he could see over the dashboard when he acted as chauffeur. We went to discotheques and clubs to see the bands that were playing and enjoyed the freedom that came with access to a vehicle.

Later, after he got his driver's license, Robert would continue the role of chauffeur while driving my father's Cadillac Fleetwood. Robert pulled up in front of a club, jumped out and opened the car door for us as my friends and I would pour out of the shiny black limousine. We made a game of pretending we were important people, when we were really just high school kids out for a good time.

Sadly, Robert got cancer and passed away when he was only 35 years old. We'd continued to be friends as we aged. He was the first friend I lost from my glory days in high school. In my youth, Robert spent more time at my house than at his own. I miss him a lot.

Colt 45 Malt Liquor was a popular drink, along with Southern Comfort, a fruit-flavored liqueur favored by young people at the time. All summer long, we took trips to the city, drank, and listened to the bands playing in clubs or at free concerts in Central Park.

Rock music was a big influence on kids back then and we were no different. I even joined a band called "The Five of a Kind, Plus One".

I played drums from 1964 to 1969. We always practiced at my house. My mother somehow put up with the noise and having my bandmates hanging around. I think she just liked knowing what her son was up to. Having us practice at home was her way of keeping an eye on things.

We'd play in battle of the band competitions, bar mitzvahs, and such events. This is where I first got comfortable up on a stage in front of people, a skill that served me well and led to many opportunities later in my life. After winning a battle, our band was invited to play at Forest Hills, in the tennis stadium. Five thousand people attended, including my group of friends who were there drinking Colt 45 out of Coke bottles. My little sister Gail was always tagging along, which was OK. She and I got along fine. Later, I made trips to bring pot to Gail and her friends in her college dormitory. I traded her pot for her girlfriends' phone numbers. My sister and I are still working together at Gimbel & Associates.

In high school, Alan and I spent a lot of time when we should have been in class hanging out at "The Rest" — a hill on the school grounds where students talked, and smoked cigarettes and pot.

Alan was my best friend in school, and we have remained close, even now. As teenagers, he and I would go to the pizza parlor to meet girls. We'd skip school and get into minor trouble, like letting the air out of teachers' tires while their cars were in the school parking lot. We were always up to something. Alan made me laugh. He was always quick with a joke.

Alan is now a sommelier and wine connoisseur. Maybe his interest in Southern Comfort led him to his appreciation for finer beverages later in life!

In high school, I got my first motorcycle, a Norton Commander 750. I loved motorcycles so much, they became the focus of my first business, which I called Cycle Exchange. My friend Richard and I brokered buy and sell transactions among other motorcycle enthusiasts and business was good. Being around motorcycles so much naturally led to some acquisitions. At one time, I had four or five bikes in my parents' garage, including a Harley and a Ducati. Sometimes sellers couldn't make a sale and just wanted to get rid of their motorcycles. I bought them at huge discounts. I remember modifying a Harley into a chopper — in the middle of my mother's living room. It took eight months, and she somehow tolerated the mess.

My friends Jeff, Carl, and I used to take car and motorcycle trips to Boston, where we knew some girls. We camped and hung out with motorcycle gangs we met along the way.

I guess I was always attracted to motor sports. At age nine, I was racing go carts. My dad was a big supporter of my interest. He'd take me to racetracks to race against people much older than me. I remember racing at Blitz Kart Stadium, whipping around the track at 50 miles per hour. Everyone thought it was great, this little kid taking on the teens and young adults on the track. My cousin, my sister, and I were even featured on the cover of Popular Karting magazine because of our young age in the sport. See the pictures at the front of the book.

One day I hit a hay bale that was supposed to keep the carts on the track. I flipped into the air, ejected from the cart, and landed prone on the track. I didn't get hurt, but that crash ended my racing career. Mom said, "no more of that!"

My parents were mostly supportive of my activities, but they came down hard when I mis-used my privileges. When I came home drunk one night and parked my Firebird on the front lawn because I couldn't find the driveway, Dad took the car away.

For the most part, my parents were willing to let me try things and learn on my own, but they were there to straighten me out if I messed up. They would have preferred that I paid more attention in school and went to class more often, but I think they understood I wasn't being lazy. I just had other things on my mind.

My preference for partying and hanging out at The Rest instead of taking school seriously gave me time to think about getting into business. Later, the education I got running a business turned out to be more valuable to me than what they were probably teaching in those classes I missed.

Like lots of kids my age, I was a marijuana consumer. I used to travel to Long Beach to buy pot from a guy named Wayne, who was quite a character and is now a Hollywood actor.

I hung out sometimes with another set of friends, Miles and John. Miles was my compadre on the Acapulco trip where I met my future wife, Cheryl. His friend John was building a resort complex in Jamaica near the Negril Cliffs. Miles and I would go there in the mid-70s and stay for weeks at a time. We'd dine at a place called Rick's Café and watch the Rastafarians get stoned and jump off the 130-foot cliff into the sea. I even did it once, somehow overcoming my fear of heights. Pot may have influenced that decision.

In 1975, I took a trip to Jamaica with Miles. We were driving a rental car, had smoked a great deal of local weed, and were both stoned. Neither of us should have been driving, but I was behind the wheel, trying to find our way back to Negril.

We came to a fork in the road. One way led to Negril, the other to Kingston.

Miles said, "Take the right fork".

"No," I said, "Negril is to the left."

"It's the right!"

"Miles, it's the left!"

We argued, and impaired as I was, I drove up the embankment.

The car flipped over, rolled down the hill, and into the ocean. Miles made it out the passenger side and I escaped through the driver's side, still holding the steering wheel that had come loose in the crash. We could have easily drowned that day. It was the closest I ever came to death.

The last we saw of it, our rental car was sinking into the sea, upside down. We watched as the wheels disappeared beneath the waves.

I emerged from the water covered in mud, including my once white jacket with no shirt, long hair, and a stylish Fu Manchu moustache, grasping the steering wheel of our rental car. Miles took one look at me and laughed hysterically at the sight.

We sat by the side of the road until some girls came by, and gave us a lift back to town. Somehow, we convinced the rental company their car had broken down at the side of the road. To my amazement, they gave us another car! I guess I was a pretty good talker even back then. I don't know if they ever discovered what really happened. When you luck out like that, you don't ask questions!

Pot wasn't a business for me. I was not a dealer. I just liked to smoke it and hang out with my fellow pot-smokers. John however, took pot a little more seriously. Besides investing in real estate, John was a smuggler. He would buy kilos of Jamaican pot and bring it back to the US. A girl he knew was a flight attendant with Jamaican Air. She'd let John load suitcases full of pot on the plane when he flew back to the states.

It got to be too risky for me. I was OK with using marijuana, but I didn't want to end up in jail for smuggling the stuff. I stopped flying back on the same plane with John.

Besides John, no one else in my group of friends were pot distributors. We were more interested in consumption and thankfully, we never got caught.

I was friendly with a different flight attendant and she and I would buy the pot in a place in Jamaica called Maroon Town. Maroon Town was a place in the hills where Vietnam draft dodgers gathered in several ganja bars. It was a remote and primitive area where pot was a prominent cultural feature. We couldn't smoke all the pot we purchased, so we made it into tea and drank it, which led to us relax to the point of almost missing our flight home. Somehow, my flight attendant friends got the airline to hold the flight until we got to the airport.

Later, I took Cheryl to Jamaica before we were married. We stayed in a place on the beach called T-Water Cottages. On the first night some guys armed with machetes came in and stole all our money, jewelry, and my camera. The law enforcement at the time was pretty laughable and we could never identify the perpetrators. It could have been much worse. Nobody was hurt, but that was our last trip to "laid back" Jamaica.

Looking back, I realize that despite all the fun and crazy things I did with my friends, they were smart guys. They were just following a different path from the traditional school, work, and family trajectory pursued by our more strait-laced schoolmates.

If there's a theme to my time as a child and young adult, it's a desire to be accepted. I can remember being worried that I wasn't good enough to be included in a group, and I wanted to make my own mark in the world. Maybe that's why I chose to do some of the things I did and hung out with my particular group of friends. For me, acceptance would not happen because of academics, so I found other ways to fit in.

The quest for acceptance and to be known for my own accomplishments definitely carried onward past my younger days. My time as a disco owner probably related to that internal desire for recognition. Later, I made a name for myself in business by making shrewd deals with big companies like AT&T and Xerox. To some degree, that aspiration for recognition continues within me to this day.

My friendship with Alan continued way past our high school and college days. After we both married and had kids, our families took cruises together. We were older and more responsible, but we still did some wacky things like borrow costumes from the on-board theater group and walk around the ship. The other passengers thought we were part of the show and we played along. One time I even wore a complete monkey suit over my own tuxedo "monkey suit" and got lots of laughs.

Alan's family and mine went sailing on our boat lots of times as well. Friendships that last almost an entire lifetime don't happen very often. I'm thankful for being able to have that with Alan.

My childhood friends had lots of influence over what I would become as an adult. I'm grateful for all the experiences I had with them.

8

. . .

1987 — 2001

The Takeover and the Towers

The breakup of AT&T created some new entities. I've already mentioned Bellcore. Another organization mandated by the government because of the antitrust action with AT&T was the National Exchange Carrier Association (NECA). NECA was a holding company created to pass phone calls through the Baby Bell companies. NECA distributed the revenue from the long-distance calls to the new independent companies. They handled billions of dollars. My company, XRC, had relationships with both Bellcore and NECA.

This was a period of high creativity in the history of our printing business. We were a much smaller company than Xerox, Pitney Bowes, or one of the other large corporations that were vying for the business opportunities made possible by the AT&T divestiture. To compete, I had to think of new, innovative approaches and ways to apply the technology of the day. We did this with innovations like XPODS, hub and spoke operations, and distributed printing networks.

In the late '90s, some outside events that would change my business and my life forever occurred. The first involved a Christian religious organization. You wouldn't think a church would have a big influence on the printing business, but it did.

In 1998, Trinity Church decided to convert all the lower Manhattan buildings they owned into high-end condominiums. Most of those buildings housed manufacturing plants. Many printers were based in Lower Manhattan, lots of them in Trinity Church properties.

To accomplish their goal, the church tripled the rent, forcing companies to move out. This action wasn't illegal, but I didn't think it was right, so I called up the New York Times. The Times printed a full page in the Sunday edition featuring me and my picture. The piece called attention to how the church was forcing my company and others out of Manhattan with a 300% price increase.

At the same time in '98, the union representing my employees decided they wanted to raise our pension contribution by 15% and increase salaries. Higher expenses would obviously impact our profit margins.

Business was fine in 1998. I still had the long-term contracts, but we no longer experienced the booming increases we enjoyed in the '80s. Things were slowing down.

Together, shrinking new business opportunities, financial pressure from the union, and the exorbitant rent increase made it clear that a new strategy was necessary if my business was to continue growing and thriving.

I was contemplating what to do about these new challenges when I got a phone call from people I knew from a group of companies known as American Laser, American Direct Mail, and Atwater Press. They had seen the Times article and knew we were getting kicked out of our space. The executives at the company said they had room in one of their facilities available for a ten-year lease. They wouldn't be facing a huge rent increase anytime soon. We could move our operation into their plant and both companies would benefit.

I met with the executives from American Laser for lunch and talked about their proposal. It sounded like a good idea. Both companies hired members of the same union, they had statement printing business which we did not, and we had the print on demand customers they lacked. The American Laser group was a $90 million per year company. Ours was about $25 million. Connecting with a bigger organization seemed to make sense, especially when facing the financial challenges ahead.

The Bellcore contracts with the minimum impressions and equipment buyout provisions made XRC an attractive prospect and the American Laser people suggested a merger. If we merged, I'd get stock in the new $130 million company, with plans to take it to $170 million.

We did a tremendous amount of due diligence, putting together all the necessary reports and accounting for asset inventory, trying to decide if a merger was a good idea. I was putting in long hours working on the merger while still running the company.

By the time we finished, we'd generated piles of documents to review. Attorneys were paid, and under pressure from our landlord and the union, we negotiated a deal. I thought I'd saved my company from the tough times those increased costs were going to create.

Unfortunately, things didn't go as smoothly as I expected. A couple of months after the merger, we started having disagreements about disclosures and other items. The American Laser partners thought we hadn't been honest about the state of our business, and we fought about the details.

It wasn't just disputes over the deal that were making me uncomfortable so soon after the merger was complete. I was a minority shareholder in the merged organization, Global Document Solutions, which was a new role for me. Since taking over my family's printing business, I'd always been in charge. I'd had the final say on strategies and business decisions. Now I lacked that level of influence, and my partners were not listening to me. I'd never been in a position where my views and ideas, as a successful industry veteran, were summarily dismissed and I didn't like it.

It took a while, but I finally realized my new partners had a hidden plan. They intended to make me miserable and force me out. The deal to which I'd agreed was a calculated takeover, not a merger.

I didn't know it when they were wooing me, but the people behind American Laser group had a history of merging with smaller organizations and then forcing the owners out. It looked like they were following the same game plan with XRC.

I'd taken a family business that my dad had started, and I had expanded, and made a deal with the devil. It was a big mistake.

The plans for business growth and the lure of personal wealth clouded my judgment. My personal income doubled the day we merged. I honestly thought this was a smart move. I was convinced I'd found a solution to the problems presented by increased costs and saved jobs for my loyal employees.

I thought I was safe because JP Morgan Bank backed the agreement with a letter of credit. If anything happened and Global Document Solutions owed me money, I could present my papers to JP Morgan, and they would pay. I wasn't relying entirely on my partner's success.

My agreement called for a five-year personal commitment. When that time was up, I could cash in and leave the company.

Two years after the merger, I hated what I was doing and had mostly shut down mentally. I'd go into the office, make a few phone calls, take a three-hour lunch, return and make another call or two and then go home for the day. The plan to get rid of me was working because I didn't want to be there.

I eventually sued my partners over our conflicts, and they sued me. I spent lots of money on attorneys. The personal relationships with my new partners evaporated. It made going to the office very uncomfortable, but I had to do it. I was contractually obligated.

Because I was a partner, I had no performance contract. My antagonists wanted to be rid of me and hated having to pay me, even if I wasn't contributing anything to the company. I took all my allotted vacation time, went to conferences, and did everything I could to not sit at the office while still satisfying the requirements of my employment. I was careful to not violate any terms of the agreement.

In September 2001, I returned to the office in New York after attending the Graph Expo trade show for a week in Chicago. I could see the World Trade Center towers from my office window. We were about ten blocks away.

On September 11th, I noticed what I thought was a small fire at one of the World Trade Center towers. When the second plane hit, we heard the enormous explosion and our entire building shook. We couldn't see the crash from our building, but we saw what happened on TV.

Three or four hours later, I got a phone call from a friend of mine from CAP Ventures. He said he was walking to my building, covered in dust and soot, and could he come in and get cleaned up. Of course, I invited him in. He'd been at the World Trade Center that morning, scheduled to give a presentation. He was one of the lucky individuals who escaped the tragedy of 9/11.

Later in the day, Global Document Solutions had a board meeting. The other board members didn't want to let the day shift go home or tell the next shift not to report for work because they'd have to pay the workers according to the union contract. I told the board I was going downstairs to tell my employees they could stay or leave, whichever they chose. I thought it was insane to make the rest of the employees keep working. At 4:00 on September 11, 2001, we thought we might be at war. The board's attitudes about their workers were a good indication of the kind of people with whom I had partnered.

My car was in the building's garage, but I didn't know how I'd get home. Authorities had blocked the roads and people couldn't get out of the city in cars. I called my friend, Sean, and asked him to go to the marina, get my boat, and come pick me up at the East River.

"Roger, I don't know how to drive your boat," said Sean.

"Find someone to help you and come get me," I pleaded. I didn't know what was going on for sure, but I wanted to be home, not at the office. Sean agreed to try, but I called him back an hour later and told him to forget it. The Coast Guard had closed the river, so getting to Long Island by water was no longer an option.

The day of the terrorist attack was the day I decided I was finished with this partnership. They had shown their true colors during a crisis and that did it for me. I decided to settle with those guys and be done with it. I was fifty years old and would have enough money to pay my bills and retire if I wanted.

I protected all my employees as much as I could and walked out the door. For the first time since my early entrepreneurial days, I had no company and no business responsibilities. I didn't even have a business card in my pocket.

I remember thinking I was now a nobody and that didn't feel very good. Much of my personal identity was connected with being a successful businessman, and that was no longer part of my life. I was burnt out and had a lot of negative feelings about the print business, but I didn't know what to do next. I got offers from other companies once word got out that I was available, but I wasn't ready to jump back into the industry where I'd spent so much energy, only to get taken advantage of.

Looking back, I can see I was fooled by only focusing on the positives of the merger. I was looking for perfection, which the deal seemed to provide: affordable space, same union, personal wealth, and opportunity. I ignored the possible pitfalls.

The statement printing business that existed in lower Manhattan essentially disappeared after 9/11 and Global Document Solutions never recovered from the loss of business. They went bankrupt seven years after I left.

The takeover experience taught me to be more careful in how I evaluate situations and carefully consider the people I want around me. I'm a tough negotiator, but always fair. Since my experience with Global Document Solutions, I am conscious of the dangers of focusing on only the positive aspects of a business deal.

9

· · ·

2001 — 2004

Takeover Complete - Moving On

I walked out of Global Document Solutions with a business entity in my name. Though I'd sold all the assets to Global, I'd kept the Electronic Reproduction Service corporation. That gave me a place to start.

The first thing I did was set up a payroll system for myself. It was important to me that my family not see any difference in the household finances, just because things turned out so badly. Using the ERS corporation, I could fund the payroll from my investments and have regular paychecks, just as before. My wife got the same kind of checks she was used to, and things proceeded normally on the home front.

Cheryl knew I'd left Global; I wasn't trying to deceive anyone. I just wanted to be sure this disappointing business venture of mine didn't cause problems for my family.

The day after I left Global, I started making calls. I wasn't sure what I wanted to do, but I was not going to sit at home wallowing in regret. I didn't have the printing company anymore, but I came out of the deal pretty well. Global still owed me money to be paid out over time and, to their credit, they made all those payments as we agreed.

Two of my first calls were to people at Xerox. I talked to two acquaintances, Tom and Frank and we made plans to get together to talk about opportunities.

I'd known Frank for years. We'd worked together when Xerox's DocuTech development project was underway, and he helped me on the XPODS project. I'd also dealt with Frank during a time when he'd left Xerox to work for a company called Indigo. Hewlett Packard eventually purchased Indigo, but this was way before that transaction took place.

When I still had the printing company before the merger, Frank had called to tell me about the new printing presses Indigo was manufacturing. He insisted that our printing company should have one. Frank had never steered me wrong as long as I'd known him. I trusted his advice and business sense. He sent me a plane ticket, and I went to meet Frank for lunch in Boston, where Indigo was based.

Lunch was at the airport and Frank walked in with a contract in his briefcase. He proceeded to tell me about the color capabilities and other features of this $600,000 printing device, promising it would change my business forever.

I bought the machine sight unseen, based on the trust I had in Frank. Once it was delivered, we installed the Indigo ePrint 1000 at Bellcore.

Interestingly, after I'd purchased the ePrint 1000 from Frank, I got a call from Xerox. They knew I'd bought the device, and they told me they had two Indigo presses they'd been testing in their labs. Testing was complete, and they wanted to sell them. Would I be interested?

I flew to a lunch meeting at Xerox headquarters in Rochester to look at the Indigos. It turned out that Xerox was preparing to go to market with a competing device, the iGen. They no longer had a use for the Indigo presses.

I could use one Indigo as a backup, but really didn't need two of them. Fortunately, I knew someone from the IPN group, Steve, who had a printing company in North Carolina. Steve was looking for an Indigo, so I left the meeting with Xerox without committing to anything and called Steve.

Steve was interested in the slightly used Indigo. I told him he'd have to wire me $200,000 quickly to take advantage of this deal. He agreed.

Back with Xerox for dinner, they asked me what I'd be willing to pay for the ePrint 1000s. I offered $200,000 for both of them. They balked, claiming the machines were worth $500,000 each. I knew this wasn't true for these two-year-old presses. I also knew, through another source, that Xerox had been attempting to sell these units for the last six months, with no takers. My negotiating position was strong.

I upped my offer to $250,000 if the deal included all the parts, paper, and shipping to two different locations. I could wire transfer the funds to them the next morning. Xerox said no. They had to get at least $500,000 for the two machines.

I thanked them for dinner, explained I had another meeting, and headed toward the restaurant exit. The Xerox people chased me down and pleaded with me to come up with a better deal. I explained that $250,000 was all I had, but I'd call my accountant. My "accountant", of course, was Steve!

I asked Steve if he could afford $250,000 if the deal included the server to run the Indigo and free shipping. "Roger," Steve said, "I haven't even seen the machine!"

"That's OK," I told him, "If it doesn't work, I'll take it back."

Returning to the dinner table, I gave Xerox my final offer; $275,000 for both machines, parts, paper, and shipping. They agreed, giving me one press for myself and another one that I sold to Steve for $250,000. The machine I kept didn't include a server, but I already had one from my earlier Indigo purchase.

Nothing about this deal was underhanded. I just took advantage of my connections and my knowledge of the industry to get a great bargain. Xerox got some money out of idle equipment they needed to dispose of, Steve got everything he needed in his North Carolina printing operation, and I got a back-up Indigo press at a fire sale price.

My friends know me as a good negotiator. They often call on me for help when they are buying things. I recall one instance when my friend Andy asked for my help buying a boat. Andy didn't know much about boats, but he'd found one on Long Island and we went together to take a look at a used boat.

The boat looked terrible. The dealer hadn't even tried to clean it. Andy was sure we'd wasted a trip. The vessel looked like a nightmare to him. I knew a lot more about boats than he, and it looked sound to me.

We talked to the dealer and negotiated a price. Andy was skeptical, but I told him, "Andy, buy the boat and get the hell out of here!" The dirt and garbage could be cleaned. He'd gotten a great deal on a good boat.

· · ·

Frank never forgot the favor I'd done him by buying a machine on faith. He later returned to Xerox, and I knew he'd help me any way he could, now that I was basically unemployed.

After my meeting with Frank, he called Tom and asked him to find something for me in his business development group. Tom understood the value of my industry knowledge and agreed to bring me on as a contractor. We agreed on a consulting contract, and I walked out of Tom's office feeling pretty good. After only a week since departing Global, I had my first contract as a consultant. This was perfect. I was ready to move away from print manufacturing. This was the beginning of something new in my life.

I wasn't sure at the time what I could do as a consultant, but I knew I had lots of industry knowledge. I could teach people, and I was a pretty good speaker. I hoped these things would help me find a new career.

One of my contacts offered me some office space for free and I started working as an independent contractor with Tom at Xerox as my only client. I started supporting the Xerox business development team by doing presentations on behalf of Xerox at places like Graph Expo and Xerox's DocuWorld event.

Eventually, I became part of a troupe of speakers at a new series of Xerox events called "Innovate". The speaker lineup included about eight of us who would tour around to different US cities and deliver content at the two-day Innovate events.

I'd spoken on the Innovate circuit for about two years when Tom asked me for ideas for a new international event series.

I had some thoughts and consulted with Roberts Communications, Xerox's advertising agency. I explained I wanted to design a program that highlighted variable data printing. We came up with a program called "Lunchinar", which we would launch at the Graph Expo trade show as a trial.

With Lunchinar, invited guests would place an order for their lunch using an online form. When they came to the Xerox booth in the exhibit hall, their custom-ordered lunch would be waiting for them. We packed each lunch in custom-printed, personalized containers. The program promoted Xerox's variable printing technology and color printers. The only problem was the expense. Feeding 500 people customized lunches wasn't in the budget.

To lower the costs, Lunchinar became "Snackinar". It was a multi-channel effort with a registration website and mailings with reply devices. Snackinar became the prototype for the new Xerox international event series. It became very successful.

Of course, I was being paid by Xerox. I was still a consultant. All this multi-channel campaign and program development work eventually became the baseline services for my stand-alone business development consulting company. I drew upon my connections and contacts to get started, and built a new business from almost nothing.

As things developed, we moved to office space on Long Island and my sister Gail joined me. Gail had tons of experience in sales from back when we had the Copy Shops and she brought her enthusiasm and creativity to this budding entity that wasn't quite a business yet.

Gail was a great salesperson. As a young woman in 1979, when few women were selling print, she sold a $1 million deal to New York Life Insurance — a huge contract for us. I've always been grateful to have my sister at my side.

I was still doing Innovate and other events for Xerox when I met Lois through Xplor International. I needed a speaker for an event I couldn't attend, and I knew Lois was an accomplished presenter. She went in my place, impressed the Xerox people, and became the first associate in what would later become a company called Gimbel & Associates. The business wasn't hugely profitable, but we were still building something I thought would be a successful and lucrative business model. Gail and Lois would soon be joined by other contractors and staff members that formed the core of a new company.

The next variable data program we created was the "Digitally Cool" program I mentioned earlier. Working with Roberts Communications again, we created personalized, multi-channel campaign elements. People who attended a Digitally Cool event received personalized brochures and raffle tickets to win prizes like digital cameras.

At a Digitally Cool presentation in India, I was standing in front of the hotel watching hundreds of people going into the building. I asked a hotel employee why all the people were there, and he told me it was for our Xerox event! It astounded me that we drew so many prospective customers. Then I started looking more closely at the people streaming by. A good many of them didn't look like they would be potential purchasers of digital printing equipment. Apparently, the invited guests turned around and invited their families to accompany them. Everyone was coming for lunch! This was a common practice in India! Only about 60 people in the group were interested in printing. Their grandparents, kids, and other relatives just came for the food. The buffet served about 600 people that day.

My group handled complete event management for Digitally Cool in cities across the globe for a year. New connections we made because of this program allowed me to expand the brand and we were asked to do even more events.

Xerox hosted Thought Leadership Workshops for commercial printers at their Gil Hatch Center in Rochester, New York. My group handled all the presentations, round tables, and interactive sessions. Included was a pirate-themed night that featured variable data maps and sent the attendees on a quest for treasure. My team and I wore full "Pirates of the Caribbean" costumes and makeup. I was "Jolly Roger" and made up to resemble Johnny Depp in his famous role.

The Thought Leadership Workshops introduced lots of printing professionals to the services we were providing to Xerox, and we signed more customers for the consulting business from these connections.

Xerox would sometimes include our business development services in the deal when they sold printing hardware. Other times, commercial printers hired us directly.

By this point in 2003, Gimbel & Associate services included industry consulting, event management, multi-channel campaigns, presentations, and business development. We began offering services to other companies, though Xerox was still our primary customer. We ran this model, growing as we went, for about ten years.

At one point, Xerox reduced their internal business development staff, and we took on much of the responsibility for that department. Many of the associates that later joined my company were former Xerox employees.

The next area we entered was training. Xerox asked us to train their sales reps in Leesburg, Virginia. We ended up collaborating with Allison who had worked at Xerox to develop the courses. Allison eventually joined my company as an associate. She is still with me at Gimbel & Associates.

The biggest advantage we had for training Xerox sales reps was my experience as a printer. I was the kind of person to whom they would be selling Xerox equipment. I could tell the sales reps exactly how to approach printers and had plenty of credibility.

We learned the industry had lots of need for training courses. Over time, people would hear about us doing one thing, and then hire us to do another. Embracing expansion was a big part of our success. This set the stage for the next ten years at Gimbel & Associates.

I love what I do now, and I like the people I work with, but I'd never have gone this route if the deal at Global Document Solutions had worked out the way I planned. I don't think I would have left the print production business and started a company that provides business development, training, and consulting. Gimbel & Associates would not exist.

Had I stayed with Global, I may have eventually done some of the same things I ended up doing as Gimbel & Associates. The marketplace was going to point us to variable data and digital printing. I might have started a professional services or business development group within Global Document Solutions if I had stayed and if 9/11 hadn't been such a blow to their statement printing business. But the events at Global turned out to be a turning point in my life that led me to something I really enjoy. They say when one door closes, another opens. That's certainly true in my case.

Instead of feeling like a nobody without a company, I realized I was still Roger Gimbel, and I had a lot to offer. People respected my opinions and knowledge, and I had the right personality and drive to make a thriving business out of a small experiment in consulting.

10

. . .

2005 — 2013

Growing the Business (and some TV fun)

B y 2005, I was doing a lot of international meetings, many of them with the International Printers Network (IPN). I was the chairman of the organization when we held our spring meeting in April 2005 in Seattle. Xerox sponsored the meeting, and we had great attendance.

During the meeting, I got a phone call from my sister Gail, who was running our yacht charter business, Hattrick Yacht Charters. The weather was warm that spring and the boat was in the water already in Montauk, New York.

In 1998, I had replaced my 30-year-old boat with a 65-foot Hatteras yacht. We continued to host fishing expeditions for business associates and started a charter company. Besides a legitimate business tool, boating was my way of relaxing, and brought in a little money too.

Gail had gotten a request, forwarded through the Montauk Yacht Club and the chamber of commerce, from a film company that wanted to use our 65-foot yacht for a TV show. I asked her who was interested, and Gail said they wouldn't tell her, but they sent a contract.

"I'm tied up in meetings," I told her, "But fax the contract to me at the hotel. I'll look it over and let you know what I think."

Two hours later, one of the hotel employees delivered the fax to me. It was enormous. Looked like a thousand pages! I couldn't figure out what they were proposing that took so much text to explain. Then I started reading, and the document was filled with every kind of non-disclosure language you could imagine, along with healthy penalties if we talked about the show before it aired on TV. It came from a guy named Mark Burnett, who was an unknown television producer at the time. Later of course, Burnett would become the Emmy winning king of reality TV, producing shows like "Survivor", "Shark Tank", and "The Voice".

At the bottom of the contract, I noticed a note that mentioned the new TV show called "The Apprentice". I'd heard about the show, but knew little of the details, so I called up Burnett. It took a while, but I finally got on a call with him and Donald Trump, who was to be the star of the show.

This was going to be great exposure for our charter company, they said. Lots of exposure in syndication across the country, they promised. They didn't want to pay to use the boat, but they'd buy some jackets and other uniform garments to outfit the crew during filming. Our benefit was the exposure on TV. This conversation occurred on a Tuesday. They wanted to film over the weekend.

I had a captain and crew available, and Gail was there to coordinate things, so I said, "What the heck. It's early in the season and we probably wouldn't be chartering the boat to anyone else, anyway." I signed the contract.

The episode of the first season of "The Apprentice", featuring our yacht, aired in October. The show awarded prizes to winning teams of contestants and the prize for one episode was a sport fishing expedition on our boat. They flew the show contestants in on a private jet and they enjoyed a clam bake at the Montauk Yacht Club after their fishing trip. A film crew captured it all. You can view the video of The Apprentice contestants on our boat at our charter company website: *https://hattrickyacht.com/about-us/*.

The charter business helped to offset the cost of keeping the vessel. The TV show thing was fun even if it didn't bring in any money. As it turned out, this was not the only time my family got involved in reality television. More on that at the end of this chapter.

In 2005 Gimbel & Associates was doing lots of presentations and building the brand. I needed to re-create myself after deciding not to be a printing company owner anymore. By this point, I had evidence that I had something to offer that people would pay for. The industry presentations, seminars, and training we were doing established my company and myself as trusted and knowledgeable industry experts.

Our target market at the beginning was printers. Having been in the business, it gave us lots of credibility with this audience. We knew about their challenges and opportunities because we'd experienced the same things.

Our competitors were other printing consultants, most of whom had never run a press or made a printing plate. My history and family printing business made Gimbel & Associates unique.

For a brief history about the business my father built, download "Gimbels in Print" from the Gimbel & Associates website: *https://www. rogergimbel.com/library*.

As we started gaining some traction, I started thinking about what else we could offer our customers. Business Development Services, Strategic Planning, and Business Plan Development became important offerings that we sold.

It wasn't unusual to find that printers had no formally documented business plan. Owners often kept a vague idea of their strategy in their heads, but they did not write it down. We showed these business owners how to profit from a more strategic approach. Demand for this kind of focused consulting was high, and we did very well by providing those services.

Strategic Assessments were another popular consulting engagement. We would assess every aspect of a printer's operation, write a report, and provide recommendations for improvement. Sometimes our customers engaged us to implement our recommendations and sometimes not.

Gimbel & Associates Sales Training evolved from the training work we did with Xerox, created by Allison after she joined our company. In sales training role-playing exercises, I would play the part of the buyer and make our customers practice selling to me. I was a tough buyer. At the end of the training, each of the printer's salespeople had to deliver a presentation to a pretend board of directors. I played the CEO. I never fired anyone like in "The Apprentice", but we gave prizes for the best presentations.

After we started training salespeople, we realized that Sales Manager Training was also necessary, so we developed a program to help managers at printing companies manage their salespeople to deliver positive results.

Marketing collateral was something sorely missing in the business strategies for many printers. Kristin from our group created examples and information to help printers market their own businesses. We didn't advertise ourselves as a marketing agency, but we had access to creative people like graphic designers who would develop brochures and other marketing materials for our clients.

Workflow Analysis, IT Infrastructure, eCommerce, and website design were other weak areas for printers in 2005. Most printers had websites, but most of them looked the same. Printers almost always featured photos of their presses on their websites. It happened so often, I started referring to the picture as "the big one" because the pictures were invariably of giant Heidelberg presses or other massive pieces of equipment. Accompanying the photos was usually a long list of other machines the printers had on their production floor.

Printing customers don't care about the equipment. They care about what it will do for them. Most of the websites we analyzed back then were not communicating value at all. Some sites like this still exist today and I cringe every time I run across them.

We showed printers how they could conduct business over the internet. We introduced our clients to software that enabled them to accept jobs online, do proofing, or even complete a transaction. We had connections and knowledge about all the companies offering such capabilities. We introduced clients to companies like Quadient, Crawford Technologies, NEPS, Sefas, and XMPie. Now, of course, our list of companies to which we refer clients is much larger.

Working with outside companies has always been a part of how Gimbel & Associates operates. We can't know every*thing*, but we know practically every*body* that can help our clients achieve their objectives and improve their businesses.

Most of the associates at Gimbel & Associates are contractors. We've always maintained a small core of key employees and called on our Associates whenever a project required their expertise. Everyone who worked in our company had actual field experience. We didn't bring on analysts or consultants that hadn't actually worked in the printing business.

Every time we brought on someone to the team, they came with skills and ideas. These people were great in areas where I had little experience. Their skills raised the value of what we were providing to our clients.

I wasn't afraid to spend money on people that were good at what they did. My strategy was to put the resources best equipped to help on a project in front of the customer. I often flew Associates across the country to make sure our clients got the help they needed from the experts who could provide it.

Our arrangements with clients were almost always annuity relationships. We'd contract to provide certain services for a certain fee. The contracts were long term and usually renewed, providing our company with a steady income stream, which allowed us to plan and grow.

Around 2008 or 2009, we began to realize the smaller printing companies that really needed our help couldn't afford us. These small businesses didn't generate enough revenue. The best we could do for this group was perform an assessment and deliver a list of recommendations, or playbook, for them to implement themselves.

We started expanding into enterprise organizations that could invest in annuity plans with us to generate long-term benefits. We started working with banks, insurance companies, colleges, and large corporations with in-plant print operations.

Sometimes we developed offerings in vertical markets for certain industries and in other cases we created programs horizontally that applied across different verticals. Human Resources, for instance, needed help with employee handbooks, onboarding documents, and other materials common across companies regardless of their industry.

As we developed new offerings, we needed presentations and materials to help market them. When the company first started, we did all this ourselves. As we grew in the mid-2000s, I began enlisting outside resources to produce the material we needed. I took the same approach as I did with the Associates — find the best people with the skills we needed and negotiate prices that recognized their expertise and value. I spent the money to do it right.

Eventually, we had a collection of forms, documents, and tools we could draw upon to deliver our services consistently across our client base. When I brought on a new Associate, we took the time to show them how to use our tools, documents, and methods. This approach strengthened the Gimbel & Associates brand. Before a client ever saw one of our reports, we reviewed it to make sure the language, appearance, and format were true to our brand.

It took me until 2011 or 2012 before I really began feeling comfortable about the business I had built. We started signing some large corporate clients with lucrative annuity contracts. It was around this time that I started talking to clients about ROI. Whatever a client spent with us, we aimed to deliver a return of two to four times more. We couldn't guarantee this result because we didn't control the management of our client's companies. But we achieved this goal with most of them.

• • •

It was in 2012 when I had my second encounter with the world of reality television. My daughter Erica was living in Manhattan and was approached by the Bravo network. Bravo was looking for six young women for a show called "Princesses of Long Island".

We filmed throughout the spring and summer of 2012 and it turned into a family affair. The film crews showed up and installed cameras and microphones in our house and they basically told us what our activities would be that day, so they matched up with their production schedule.

Cameras followed Erica wherever she went — shopping in the city, to the clubs, on the yacht, and in our home.

Characters in reality TV don't have scripts, but the events that make it onto the show are definitely staged. The TV people coerce and prod to create conflict and drama. The show creates situations they can film, but they don't tell the actors what to say.

Another thing I learned about reality television is that even though they were filming me and my family, we never got to see the results. Editing can set moods, create drama, or persuade an audience to feel emotion. The producers put those techniques to use on this show.

It wasn't until the morning of the day a show was to air that we received a FedEx package containing a video of the finished episode. This was a year after filming. By then I couldn't remember what we did or said, so it was always a surprise to watch the tape.

In one episode, the princesses were coming to my house for a barbecue. This was filmed in the morning. At 7:30 AM I was grilling hamburgers and frankfurters in the backyard, pretending it was the afternoon.

I had all the food laid out on the counter, getting ready to cook. Erica and my wife were in the kitchen and Erica said, "Dad, you have to serve Kosher meat. Chanel is Kosher!" Chanel was one of the other princesses.

"Well, I'll just do what the Rabbi does," I said, and I said a little prayer over the meat.

A year later, I'd forgotten all about that comment. It was caught on film, as was everything when the film crew was on site. Three and a half million people across the country saw the episode and some of them didn't like my little joke, but the meat was Hebrew National hot dogs, so I was using Kosher products all along. We didn't feed Chanel non-Kosher meat.

I got hate mail and phone calls. My Rabbi called me up. Later, people would recognize me and mention my barbecue faux pas. People on planes would ask me what was going to happen next, which of course I had no idea, considering it was filmed a year in advance and heavily edited.

The whole thing was a little too open. Everyone I knew was watching the show and making comments to me. The show didn't always paint people in the best light, which I guess was the point. Who would watch if there was no conflict or drama?

Erica was a recognizable celebrity while the show ran. She had five million Twitter followers. Everywhere she went, she was a star.

We spent the summer of 2012 filming "The Princesses of Long Island" and the next year, 2013, dealing with the changes in our lives as the show aired on Bravo. The show only ran one season and Erica didn't pursue an acting career, but it was certainly an interesting experience. Today, Erica is married to Jordan, has a three-month old son, and is excited being a new mom.

11

• • •

Expanding Our Reach and Fun with Boats

By 2013, Gimbel & Associates was concentrating on refining our sales training modules. We developed a framework that delivered results for our customers, who included both printing companies and equipment manufacturers.

Over the course of five days, we taught salespeople skills they would need to create and deliver effective sales presentations. Then we'd separate the class into groups of three. Each person in the group had a role in completing their assignment — to build and make a sales presentation. We did lots of role-playing, but we left it up to the groups to decide how they would structure their presentations. Some groups included videos; others brought in outside subject matter experts. It was entirely up to them.

I usually played the role of a print buyer, and I could be pretty critical. This was on purpose. The point of the training was not to make salespeople feel good, but to make sure they learned how to be effective at selling their company's products and services. At the end of the training, each group would get up and make a one-hour presentation to me. The best ones would win a prize, based on the opinions of the entire class.

We still use the same model today to train large groups of salespeople.

Gimbel & Associates created materials, programs, and processes that we could easily replicate from one customer to the next. If they were all in the same industry, we had a solution for them. If they shared a function across industries, we served them as well.

2013 was also a year of distractions from my business activities. My 88-year-old mother's heart problems worsened. My sister Gail and I spent lots of time taking Mom to doctors and hospitals.

Gail was living with my mom and looked after her day-to-day, and I helped whenever I could. The entire year was filled with lots of personal tasks and concerns that naturally distracted from the business goals I wanted to accomplish.

My mom passed away in 2013 at age 89. After that, with fewer ties to New York, I bought a home in Delray Beach, Florida. I thought I would sell my house in New York and move full-time to Florida. I never did, but I kept the house. My family visits Delrey Beach for short periods of time during the winter. The locals in Florida call us "snowflakes" because we don't stay long like the "snowbirds" that relocate to Florida for the entire winter.

Around this time, I put together a fishing group with some friends that included Tom (my boat captain), my friends Randy and Dennis, and myself. We did lots of fishing out of Montauk, and this group still gets together for fishing expeditions. I still had the 65-foot Hatteras yacht, which we used for the fishing group along with charters and pleasure cruising. In 2017, I bought a 40-foot center-console boat with three outboard engines that we used exclusively for fishing. I named this vessel "Midnight Express".

The boats and fishing have always been something I enjoyed. The charter business brought in some money that offset the cost and allowed me to pursue my hobby.

At the end of 2014 and beginning of 2015, print equipment manufacturers began bringing inkjet presses to the marketplace. The early models produced print less expensively than offset and toner machines, but the print quality was far below what most printers considered acceptable. We called the inkjet output "low-end business color".

Our customers were interested in what inkjet could do for their businesses, though, and we saw the potential. I gave a keynote speech at the Inkjet Summit conference in 2015 and Gimbel & Associates began to study inkjet technology in depth.

It wasn't long before my team became experts on the different inkjet technologies the equipment manufacturers were developing. We got familiar with the substrates that different machines would support, ink variations, and the benefits or drawbacks of each inkjet press available for sale. At that time, all the presses were roll-to-roll or roll-to-sheet. Production-level sheetfed inkjet presses were yet to be brought to market.

These early days of commercial inkjet printing featured lots of limitations. We saw some applications where the technology was a good fit, such as shops that produced consistently high volumes of similar print. The technology was not ready for shorter run applications, jobs that required different paper stocks, or higher quality print, but we could see the potential. We set out to offer inkjet advisory services to the marketplace.

We began telling customers how to use inkjet, how to sell it, how to incorporate it into an existing workflow, and how to assess which projects to transfer from toner or offset presses. We spent lots of time understanding what we thought would be the next big thing in the printing business.

As the technology advanced, the print quality improved dramatically, and substrate choices expanded. Many printers skipped the traditional conversion from offset to toner before investing in inkjet and instead went directly from offset to inkjet. Seeing this trend, some manufacturers reconfigured their base toner presses to use inkjet instead. They added inkjet heads and dryers and removed components they didn't need, such as fusers or developers.

Managing the transition to inkjet became an important niche for Gimbel & Associates as more printing companies and in-plant print operations began considering inkjet as an addition or replacement for their existing printing devices.

Later, cut-sheet inkjet devices expanded the number of applications that could transition to inkjet, along with widening the pool of potential inkjet press buyers. We estimated the market for inkjet devices increased six-fold with the introduction of high quality cutsheet inkjet presses. This meant more printing companies were looking for expert help as they prepared to add inkjet presses to their operation. Gimbel & Associates was the number one resource available to them.

Developing concurrently with the explosion in inkjet adoption was a rush by marketers to exploit the low cost of digital messaging. Digital marketing became so overused that it lost its impact. Many marketers eventually returned to direct mail as an important part of their multi-channel marketing strategies.

The developments in inkjet are perfectly suited to meet the needs of direct mail marketers because of the segmentation and personalization capabilities these devices can offer. Printers are replacing "spray and pray" techniques with targeted, personalized direct mail.

Personalized printing wasn't a new concept in 2015. Way back in 2003, I was already talking about the value of variable data and targeted messaging. I co-authored a book called "Individualized Media Essentials" that showed printers how to take advantage of these new techniques and technologies. Xerox bought the rights to this book. It became part of the "Xerox Profit Accelerator Toolkit" that Xerox provided to customers to help them get the most benefit from their investment in digital printing technology.

Xerox's license eventually expired, and I updated the book in 2015. In 2021, I re-wrote the book again. I've been an advocate for personalized printing for a long time!

By 2017, Gimbel & Associates started focusing on acquiring more long-term contracts. We still did what I thought of as transactional projects — those will always be part of the mix. But we turned our attention to the benefits that the longer engagements provided. I'd rather have 30-40 projects with large, continuous clients than 300 one-off projects. By 2017, we'd doubled our business. In 2018, we signed several five or six-year agreements, solidifying the stability of our workload and creating a predictable revenue stream.

The business growth my company experienced in the last half of the decade made me stop and take notice. This thing I'd started with an idea that I'd maybe work on it a couple of years before moving on had become a thriving, successful business. We were a well-established brand within the printing industry and known as experts. Many printing companies and industry vendors relied on us for guidance, training, and advice.

Plus, we had almost no competition. The competitors we had were smaller. Most of them were single, independent consultants. They could not take on a large number of projects at once like we could with our group of associates. The competing consultants also lacked the breadth of experience and knowledge we could bring to a client.

It was time for a decision. I had the house in Florida, two boats, and a charter company in addition to Gimbel & Associates. What would I do now? Should I sell the house in New York and move south? My daughter lived in Florida, so I'd see her more often if I moved, but did I want to give up on what Gimbel & Associates had become?

On the other hand, I wondered if this was the time in my life to be expanding a business. Maybe I should think about retirement.

I enjoyed what I was doing and really liked the customers and team with whom I got to work. I noticed when I called my retired friends, they didn't really have much to talk about. They spent their days at the pool or playing golf, but their lives seemed to me to be lacking a purpose. Maybe that's the way retirement is supposed to be, but I wasn't sure I was ready to live that kind of life.

Boating had always been an important activity, since going out with my father from the age of five. Cruising and fishing were constants that played parts in all areas of my life, including family time, friends, personal relaxation, and business. Any decision I made about my future was going to include this activity.

In September 2018, I asked Captain Tommy to look for a replacement for the 65-foot Hatteras. It was getting old and, just like aging printing equipment, costing more to maintain every year. I told Tommy to look for something newer and a little bigger, maybe 70 feet.

He went to Florida to look at a boat we found on the internet. It was bigger than I planned, at 85 feet, but it seemed like something worth investigating.

Tommy called me and told me he'd found the perfect boat and encouraged me to fly down and look at it. It was a beautiful boat that had been totally re-furbished. It was in great shape — I thought.

The sea trial didn't go so well. We had problems with the engines and other issues. From September to February, we did three sea trials, trying to see if this yacht was worth the investment. I really liked the boat.

The company that owned the boat originally had a contract with the US Government to use it as a training site for Navy SEALs. The vessel at one time had a huge diving platform on the back. The luxury interior had been removed and replaced with bunks to accommodate the number of men expected to occupy the boat during training exercises.

Unfortunately for the owners, they somehow lost the Navy contract before the boat ever got a chance to leave the dock. As it was configured for Navy use, the boat was un-sellable. The owner's only choice was to rip out all the military features and restore the boat to its original luxury yacht condition. It took them 2 years, and they were eager to sell.

I decided to try to make a deal for the boat even though it was twenty years old and had not fared well in the early tests.

We couldn't trade in the 65-foot Hatteras. The seller didn't want it. I ended up donating it to the National Save the Sea Turtle Foundation. I gave them the boat. They gave me a plaque, and the government gave me a tax credit.

We bought the 85-foot boat in February 2019, titled under the charter company. I flew down to Florida and Tommy and I brought the boat to New York on a seven-day trip. Now I take the boat to Florida every fall and bring it back in the spring.

The boat is all set up for working when I need to. I participate in conference calls and video chats, I have internet connections, and a comfortable place to work. This makes it much easier to take a trip, even if I have important meetings or other work to do. Business doesn't stop when I'm on my boat. See a picture of the boat on the last page of this book.

As before, we use this boat for business, charter, and personal use. I'm happy I did it.

The new boat was instrumental in my decision to stay with the business. I decided I was enjoying life too much to retire, and the yacht was a big part of it. It brought balance to my life.

In the time between the takeover of my printing business in 2001 until early 2019, everything changed for me. In 2019, I wasn't doing what I'd always thought would be my life's work. I wasn't even the same person as I was when running the printing company. Back then, I could see no other path. Funny how it turned out.

Throughout this whole ordeal, walking away from the printing business, exploring different options with Xerox, traveling all the time, losing my mom, and buying boats, my wife Cheryl has been a steadying and understanding influence in my life. The old saying that behind every successful man stands a woman sounds dated and sexist today, but in my case, it's true.

Across decades, Cheryl made sure the household ran smoothly, looked after the children, and provided me a steady base to come home to. What I have accomplished in my life took lots of time and hard work. I couldn't have endured without my wife's love and support.

More than anything, my experience with Gimbel & Associates taught me the value of working <u>on</u> the business instead of working only <u>in</u> the business. We're trying new things that will lead to expansion, but I don't have to work sixteen hours a day just to keep the business running. I've surrounded myself with trustworthy, talented people who have fantastic ideas. This allows me to take a step back from time to time and take out the boat.

I know that if something drastic happens again, it will be fine. I can always change and do something different if I want — I've already done that once.

12

. . .

2020 — 2021

Dealing with the Pandemic

2020 started out by taking the new boat to Bimini and Chub Cay in The Bahamas. In January, we were fishing and cruising. We had a timeshare in St. Thomas where I met up with my old friend Alan, who was still a jokester. Alan was watching the ships coming into St. Thomas harbor and told me he thought they were renaming one of the ocean liners "COVID of the Seas". It was funny then — we didn't know about the seriousness of the pandemic at this early stage.

When we arrived back in New York around February 25th, we found out the world had changed. By March, everything we used to do in business or for fun stopped happening. Companies shut down, people had to figure out how to work from home, and a bunch of acquaintances got sick. As you may recall, New York was the original hot spot for the disease in the US. The city's hospitals were overwhelmed, and authorities imposed severe restrictions to protect the citizens from something brand new and mostly unknown.

By March, all Gimbel & Associates' customers were working from home, and we had to adapt to communicating with them only through Zoom or other online channels. Suddenly gone were speaking engagements, conferences, and lunch meetings. Obviously, our practice of entertaining customers and partners on the boats came to an immediate halt. These in-person activities had always been an important part of doing business, and now they were gone. Nobody knew for how long.

Our customers were facing challenges of their own and they called Gimbel & Associates for advice. They had labor issues with staff members out sick with the disease or caring for family. They too faced new business challenges when they couldn't personally interact with their customers. When they did have work to do, getting it done while maintaining social distance could be tricky. The printing industry relies on some rather large pieces of equipment and multiple operators. Finding ways for people to work while staying six feet apart wasn't easy. Some in-plant print operations couldn't do it and they started outsourcing their work.

Opportunities for printers were available in some sectors. COVID-related signage and personal protective equipment (PPE) were options for some. Those who had already established a web-based storefront did better than those less prepared.

Fortunately, even though our business methods changed radically, our company stayed strong throughout the shutdowns. We grew our business by helping our customers find solutions that would allow them to operate during this difficult and transitional time.

By early 2021, we began to see the hybrid model of working, where people spent some days at home and some in the office or plant, as the new normal. Business travel lagged and didn't really start picking up until the fall of 2021 but was still at a level far below what existed pre-pandemic. Even after tests and vaccinations became more available, many companies continued to restrict access to their facilities. At some companies, only employees could enter the building — no outsiders were allowed.

I think from now on, more companies will outsource their printing. COVID-19 accelerated a trend that was already developing. We'll see more in-plant print centers shut down because the onsite operations they used to support have moved to a virtual model.

I'm writing this book towards the end of 2021 and Print-as-a-Service is on the horizon. Instead of selling print jobs, printers will help their customers design systems and programs that use print to solve business problems.

In-plant print operations may decide to run some critical jobs on-site, while they outsource everything else. This is similar to the Bellcore operation we set up back in the '90s. Other in-plants will decide they don't want to be in the printing business at all. They will outsource all their work.

Direct mail is seeing a resurgence in interest. Marketers recognize that the performance of email and other digital channels diminishes from overuse and avoidance mechanisms like spam filters and ad blockers. Successful direct mail will be increasingly targeted, personalized, and take advantage of all the capabilities of variable data and digital printing.

At Gimbel & Associates, we've been helping our customers exploit the benefits of variable data printing for a long time, using software called XMPie. I recall one campaign we designed for a veterinary company. We targeted families that had moved into an area serviced by the company and had a pet. The direct mail was addressed to the pet and included a photo of the breed of animal that lived in the household. It was very successful. We're still designing variable data projects for our customers and expect demand to continue at high levels.

The print technology of today can make any printed item personalized or targeted and produce it with high-quality inkjet or toner print devices. This includes packaging, labels, and transactional documents. The value of a printed piece must grow from its present position. Each piece must have an impact.

I coined the phrase "In the future, we in the print industry will not be judged by the quality of the output, we'll be judged on the quality of the outcome." Print companies that understand this concept will succeed. Those that do not will be left behind to run low-profit jobs or eventually cease operations.

I see 2022 as a time when business will gradually return to a level of productivity to which we are accustomed. International travel will still be restricted, which will continue to affect business. Companies that can do business within the USA will find plenty of opportunities if they keep up with emerging technologies and trends.

Travel restrictions and virus exposure concerns will challenge the International Printers Network, as it relies heavily on in-person events. People will struggle to continue supporting organizations if the benefits diminish.

Changes forced by COVID will permanently affect attendance at in-person conferences and events. We expect some of them to cease operations or downsize for smaller audiences.

Overall, I am optimistic about the future of the print industry. I think we'll see new opportunities that we haven't even discovered yet.

My father taught me to always be looking at where we were, where we are, and where we're going. I still use his advice today. At my company, we spend lots of time studying new technologies and advancements, so we're ready to help our customers understand how it works and how to use it to their advantage.

Automation will play an important part in how print evolves because print is a slow-moving medium. Someone must carry it from one place to the next. The place to speed up the process is in the design and production of print. Automation will enable this acceleration.

The cost of processing a print order today ranges between $25 and $50. It's expensive to process small orders. Technology that enables print companies to combine jobs or automate the process to slash operating overhead will have an immediate impact on the bottom line.

Printers have always viewed software as too expensive. They are hesitant to make an investment, unable to see the benefits like they can visualize with a piece of equipment. But not investing in software that improves productivity, adds capabilities, or lowers costs is more expensive than doing without — especially when the industry is changing so dramatically.

13

· · ·

What's Next?

Next for me is continued development of the many services that Gimbel & Associates provides its customers, along with some exciting new ventures.

One thing is certain. I'm not planning to retire anytime soon. I'm enjoying what I do and the people with whom I get to work every day and I'm excited about the changes coming for the print industry. Why would I leave?

ACKNOWLEDGEMENTS

It may sound strange, but I'd like to thank my partners at Global Document Solutions that took my family business from me. Despite their selfish weaknesses and a desire to get rid of me, they forced me to reinvent myself. They pushed me in a direction that turned out to be extremely good for me.

These men convinced me of my personal value, even as they tried to squash it. Their actions led me in a direction I never would have imagined.

To all my friends and associates in the industry, thank you for your support and encouragement during some stressful times in my life. I owe a huge debt of gratitude. These people, too many to name, showed me the knowledge I'd gained over many years in the print business had value. They showed me I could use the things I knew in ways much different from personally managing the process of putting ink on paper.

A special thanks to all my IPN friends across the world. You expanded my horizons and showed me that we're all printers at heart, regardless of where we live or what language we speak.

I'm fortunate to have been able to work with some of the brightest people in the business. All the people who have worked for me throughout the years, at Gimbel & Associates and before, were the real engine that pulled the train. I had the ideas and made the deals. They made everything happen.

The transition I made in my life from the early years through the takeover of the business and on to the company I built would have been impossible without support from my wife Cheryl, my sister Gail, and the rest of my family. They had faith and always had my back.

I'll always be grateful to Tommy, my boat captain, who enables me to get away from the city and spend the time on the water, which I cherish.

Decades of friendship and support came from a large group of New Yorkers — Andy & Cheryl, Jimmy & Gail, Larry & Melanie, Wayne & Helen, Mark & Andrea, Steve & Genie, Alan & Esther, Alan & Terry, and Yossi & Beth.

To my Montauk friends Gary & Deana, John & Sue, Randy & Judy, and Glen & Deborah, and my Florida friends Peter & Joyce, Joel & Janice, Ron & Sue, Mark & Felicia, and Carl & Patty, thank you for all the great times and fellowship over the years.

Thanks to Mike Porter at Print/Mail Consultants for his help putting this book together. Mike organized my collection of memories and thoughts and turned them into a readable narrative.

I titled this book after a song written by Paul Anka and recorded by Sammy Davis Jr. The lyrics to the song include the lines "I'm not any man designed to fit someone's plan. I have my own desires of the things a man aspires." That pretty much sums up my story as I see it.

If you'd like to listen to the song, search for it on YouTube. It's always been one of my favorites.

The Hattrick Yacht